AUSTRALIA WIDE

AUSTRALIA WIDE

with Bill Peach

from the second ABC television series
Peach's Australia ⦿

Published by The Australian Broadcasting
Commission in association with The
Department of Environment, Housing
and Community Development,
and Hodder and Stoughton (Australia).

National Library of Australia card number
and ISBN 0 642 97211 7

Printed and bound in Australia by Wilke
and Company Limited
37-49 Browns Road, Clayton, Victoria.

Typesetting by Photoset Computer Service
Pty Limited, Sydney

Designed by Judy Hungerford

ABC stills by Richard Walker, Richard Corfield, Kathie Atkinson,
Lloyd Capps, and John Cox.
Other stills by Robert Edwards.

Illustrations on page 39 reproduced by courtesy of South Australian
Archives. Illustration on page 36 reproduced by permission of Mitchell
Library, Sydney.

Text type 12 on 13 Baskerville.

cover: **Australia's real Outback, The Birdsville Track.**

pages 2 and 3: **Twofold Bay, scene of Ben Boyd's adventures.**

pages 6 and 7: **on the Birdsville Track.**

CONTENTS

FOREWORD

I hope that anyone who wonders why we called this book *Australia Wide with Bill Peach* will soon see why when they read the book. Australia is a very large country, equal in area to Europe and almost as big as the United States. To make the ABC television series *Peach's Australia*, we travelled the equivalent of five times around the world.

This book is based on the programs in the second series of *Peach's Australia* and the topics traverse the country from Arnhem Land in the north of the continent to Macquarie Harbour in the south of Tasmania, and from Sydney on the eastern seaboard to Fremantle on the western seaboard. Within those points of the compass can be found an astonishing variety of climate and geography, from tropical jungle to ice-clad mountains, from towering ranges to level plains, from big cities to unpopulated deserts.

Australia is the only nation to occupy an entire continent, but that does not mean that the country is all the same. For anyone who cares to look, there is a fascinating diversity in its regions and its peoples. The cattlemen on the Birdsville Track and the weekend tourist to the Dandenongs share the same continent, but they live in different worlds. An Arnhem Land Aborigine's view of Australia is not the same as a Cornish miner's. Everywhere in Australia people's lives and outlooks have been shaped by their own peculiar history and geography. There is, as a result, no such thing as a 'typical Australian'; the most you could say is that there are Australians who are typical of their own regions and cultures.

Except that it sounds a bit funny, we might have called this book *Australia Long*. Australia's recorded history is short if we think of history only as words printed on paper, published in books like this one. But the human history recorded on the rocks of Australia, in the form of paintings, is as long as any the world knows, while the geological history that is recorded in the Australian landscape dates back to the dawn of primitive life on this planet.

At that time Australia, in its size, shape and climate, was a country quite unlike anything that the white man has ever known. In the day of Australia's history, the white man has occupied only a few minutes since Governor Phillip arrived with his band of convicts. But even in that brief time this country has produced compelling stories of courage and brutality, humour and despair, great enterprises and grotesque mistakes.

All of it, black man's history, white man's history, even the history of the primitive jellyfish that swam in the ancestral ocean of Panthalassa when it washed the shores of Gondwanaland, is our distinctive past. We can't change it, but we can learn from it.

We *have* learned, slowly, to treat this country with the respect it demands, and we have achieved a more decent, just, humane and free society than the one that was imported to Botany Bay in 1788. But we still have a long way to go, and, unlike the Panthalassa jellyfish, we may not have a long time to get there.

Personal Acknowledgments

In my first book about Australian history, *Peach's Australia*, I wrote that too many people had worked on the production of the original ABC television series of the same name for me to be able to thank them all individually. I intend to correct that omission in this book, and in addition to all those people whose help I acknowledged in my first book, I want to name and thank the people who were regular members of the unit during the second series — cameraman Preston Clothier, assistant cameraman Richard Walker, unit managers Richard Corfield and Kinsie McDonald, production assistants Cathie Shirley, Geraldine Moore and Astrid Friedericks, sound men Peter Lipscomb and David Norton-Smith, editors Stan Moore and Brian Nicholls, secretary Gisela Moore.

The book *Peach's Australia* has been a huge success, and naturally I hope that *Australia Wide* will follow in its footsteps. I would like to claim that all this is because of my sheer brilliance as an author, but I know that it isn't so. The quality and popularity of the television programs have created the audience for my books, and I acknowledge that fact and thank the people whose skill made those programs successful. I also want to thank the Department of Environment, Housing and

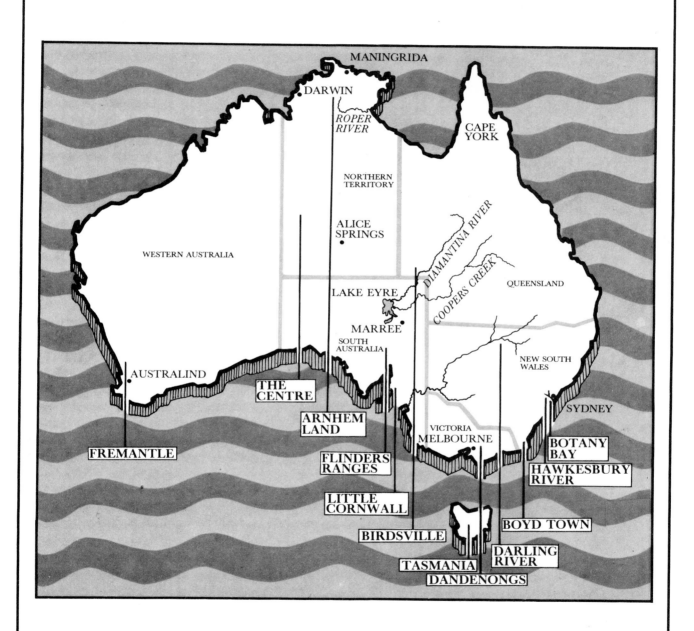

Community Development, and in particular John Womersley, for thoughtful and constructive assistance in making the series.

A film script, of course, is not a book. In fact, most documentary film scripts would be quite incomprehensible as books. The picture tends to dictate the script, and the words don't make a lot of sense when they're not allied to the original moving pictures. Therefore I have had to return to the original research and recast those stories in a way that I hope makes sense. I wish to acknowledge the help of those people who provided the original information on which this book is based: Alan Bateman, Bill Steller, Lloyd Capps and David Roberts, who directed the television programs in the second series of *Peach's Australia*, also researched their topics; Sandra Hall, Margaret Murphy, Michael Berry, Leone Adams, Helen Birch, Graham Shirley, Phil Rodwell and the late George Farwell all helped to provide the research which made *Australia Wide* possible.

Finally, I must mention that the many people I interviewed during the television series (and they *are* too numerous to list) were a mine of information. I have done a modicum of research myself — sources are quoted in the book, and there is a check list of selected reference works at the end — and my wife Shirley, as well as aiding with research, and running Peach Towers during my absences on location, has once again outshone the labours of Hercules by typing this manuscript from my ancient Etruscan calligraphy.

To her, to Peg McGrath who helped translate my abominable handwriting into print, to Louise Cook who typed the transcripts of the television programs, and to the photographers who shot the stills for this book, my heartfelt thanks.

Bill Peach.

opposite: **The shores of Botany Bay**

BOTANY BAY

William Dampier, the first Englishman to land on the coast of Australia, was a pirate — an interesting coincidence, in view of the style of Englishman later sent out to populate Botany Bay. Dampier's landing point was, however, a long way from Botany Bay. It was at the other side of the continent then known as New Holland. Dampier arrived at Buccaneer's Archipelago on the north-west coast on January 4, 1688.

Like the Dutchmen who'd landed on that barren coast before him, Dampier concluded that there was no good to be done there. In his 1698 narrative, *A New Voyage Round the World,* he gave the country such a bad report that English explorers stayed well away for nearly a century after his visit. Dampier described New Holland as a vast tract of sand, devoid of water, fruit-bearing trees or useful animals, and infested to the most hideous degree by flies. As for the native inhabitants, his description of them was pure derision:

'The *Hodmadods* of *Monomatapa,* though a nasty People, yet for Wealth are Gentlemen to these; who have no Houses and Skin Garments, Sheep, Poultry, and Fruits of the Earth, Ostrich Eggs, & c. as the *Hodmadods* have: and setting aside their humane shape, they differ but little from Brutes.'

Dampier toyed with the idea of approaching New Holland by way of Cape Horn, a journey which would have brought him to the east coast of the continent, and perhaps changed his view of it. But he never acted on the idea, and it was exactly one hundred years after his landfall in the West that the British founded in the East a society in many respects less humane and more brutish than Dampier had observed amongst the natives that he called 'the miserablest people in the world'.

Captain James Cook, after observing the transit of Venus from Tahiti, sailed on in the *Endeavour* into the South Pacific, rounded both islands of New Zealand, and on April 20, 1770, sighted the east coast of Australia. To the surprise of all on board, it did not look at all like the hellish country Dampier had described. It was covered with bushes and green grass, and well-timbered mountains were visible inland from the coast.

Cook sailed north, mapping the coastline as he went, and on April 28, 1770, with his botanists Joseph Banks and Dr Solander and a Tahitian native, he attempted to land on the Illawarra coast, north of a place the natives called Wollongong, or 'song of the sea'. On that day it happened that the sea was singing too boisterous a song and Cook, fearful of capsizing his boat in the surf, returned to the *Endeavour* and sailed on north. So Illawarra, by a freak of weather, lost its chance to become the first landing place of the great explorer.

On the next day Cook found an anchorage in what he described as 'a capacious, safe and convenient harbour'. He named the headlands of this harbour for his botanists — Cape Solander on the south, Cape Banks on the north. He had more trouble in deciding on a name for the harbour itself. His first choice was Sting-Ray Harbour, because his men captured some monstrous stingrays. Then, influenced by the delight of Banks and Solander in their botanical discoveries, he toyed with the names Botanist Harbour and Botanist Bay. Finally, at the end of his week's stay, Cook settled on the name Botany Bay — a pretty and apparently innocent name which was to gather an infamous ring in years to come through its association with the convict system.

At the time of Cook's arrival Botany Bay was a green and pleasant place and well deserving of the euphonious name he gave it. Cook himself recorded enthusiastic impressions of the meadows, the rich soil and the trees. Apparently, there were plenty of big trees — bangalays, cabbage-tree palms and eucalypts. Banks and Solander found trees and plants which had never been described by European botanists including the various types of eucalypts and the banksia. They sighted wonderful flocks of cockatoos and lorikeets and caught glimpses through the bush of strange animals unlike anything they had seen before.

Even more strange to these eighteenth century Europeans were the people of Botany Bay, the 'Indians' as Banks called them. Cook had nothing but good intentions towards these native people and fervently hoped for harmonious relations with them, but it was a meeting of two alien civilisations. One had occupied the country for thousands of years;

the other for a matter of days. Peace was not to be the result.

Many accounts of Captain Cook's arrival, until quite recent times, gave the impression that he discovered Australia. Of course he did nothing of the kind. Numbers of white men had previously encountered the southern continent, and we shall never know the name of the first black man or woman who stepped on to Australian soil perhaps forty thousand years ago. But we do know that the area where Cook landed had been occupied for some six thousand years by a Water People called the Gwea Gal. They were a fishing tribe who lived on the seashores, and in earlier times, when the ocean level was lower at the end of the Ice Age, they probably occupied lands east of Botany Bay which are now under water.

Middens can still be inspected in the sand dunes at Kurnell which reveal something of the lifestyle of these people. They ate all kinds of shellfish, including mud oysters from the bay and pippies from the beach, and in the turban shell they found not only good food but material from which they fashioned a curved and pointed fish hook. The Water People invented the fish hook about a thousand years ago. Even before that, they had another fish-catching device which was a straight piece of bone, pointed at both ends. They tied a line around the middle of this fragment and baited it. When the fish swallowed it, the fragment would turn and stick sideways in its throat.

The middens that reveal this history are in sand dune country now, but it was not sand dune country when Cook first saw it. It was forest, abounding in game which the natives were adept at catching. In fact the whole area was a natural paradise for a hunting and fishing tribe and the Water People were probably healthier and better nourished than many of the Europeans who first surveyed them from the deck of the *Endeavour*.

Several parties of natives were out fishing in their canoes when the *Endeavour* sailed into Botany Bay. Cook and his sailors were astonished to observe that the natives apparently took no notice of this strange arrival in their midst but kept their heads down over their fishing lines. Looking back at it now, it was perhaps the most poignant moment in Australian history. The Aborigines had never before seen a ship like the *Endeavour*, nor such people as stood on its deck, with their white faces and strange uniforms. Some instinct more powerful than natural curiosity must have warned the Aborigines to avert their eyes from this apparition in the harbour. It may have been the premonition that something or somebody was about to shake their world to its foundations. All they wanted was for the strange vessel to be gone. If they ignored it, perhaps it would go and leave them in peace.

But Cook did not intend to go, not yet, and he began an adventure which was to leave Aboriginal society not in peace but in pieces. His mental struggle as to what to name the bay was not the only conflict that accompanied Cook in Botany Bay. With his attempt to land, the place became a battleground. It has been, in various ways, a battleground ever since.

Isaac Smith, a young midshipman who was Captain Cook's wife's cousin, was the first white man to set foot on the shores of Botany Bay. Cook said to him, 'Isaac, you shall land first'. The courtly tone of this little ceremony was interrupted by the Aborigines, who had decided it was time for action. Two of them rushed to the rocky outcrop on the southern shore of the bay to oppose the landing of the longboat. They threw stones and brandished spears and shouted in a language the sailors couldn't understand. The sailors shouted back in a language the Aborigines couldn't understand. Finally, Cook's men decided to resolve the situation by giving the natives something they could understand — a blast of musket-shot. It was, to use the jargon of modern diplomacy, the first 'meaningful exchange' between white man and black man at Botany Bay and it set the standard for the dialogue between these two peoples which was to follow in the succeeding century.

Cook sailed away from Botany Bay after one week with two impressions predominant in his mind. One was a favourable impression of the Aborigines. That seems surprising, in view of his inability to establish any real relationship with them. But Cook was not a man of the conquistador mentality, and he could see that the Botany Bay natives enjoyed certain

top: **Cook's landing place, Botany Bay**

above: **Captain Cook's Memorial, Kurnell**

advantages which European civilisation could not bestow on them. Their tools were bad, their houses mere hovels and their canoes mean. But, he added:

'From what I have seen of the Natives of New Holland, they may appear to some to be the most wretched people upon Earth, but in reality they are far happier than we Europeans; being wholly unacquainted not only with the superfluous but the necessary Conveniencies so much sought after in Europe, they are happy in not knowing the use of them. They live in a Tranquillity which is not disturb'd by the Inequality of Condition; The Earth and sea of their own accord furnishes them with all things necessary for life, they covet not Magnificent Houses, Household — stuff & c., they live in a warm and fine Climate and enjoy a very wholesome Air, so that they have very little need of Clothing and this they seem to be fully sencible of, for many to whome we gave Cloth & c to, left it carlessly upon the Sea beach and in the woods as a thing they had no manner of use for. In short they seem'd to set no Value upon any thing we gave them, nor would they ever part with any thing of their own for any one article we could offer them; this in my opinion argues that they think themselves provided with all the necessarys of Life and that they have no superfluities.'

It was a notably more sympathetic verdict on the Aborigines than Dampier had given, and it conveyed an obvious conclusion that such people stood to gain nothing from the introduction of European civilisation.

But they were soon to have it whether they wanted it or not. For the other important impression that Cook brought away from Botany Bay was of a region of deep black soil and fine meadows, capable of growing any kind of grain.

Cook was notably more cautious in his final summing-up of Australia; and although he had raised the English flag and claimed possession of the eastern coast, which he named New South Wales, he did not suggest that the English should occupy New South Wales.

Joseph Banks, however, was not so retiring, and when the American Revolution made it impossible for Britain to send its overflow of convicts to America, Banks unhesitatingly recommended a new convict destination — Botany Bay. He told a House of Commons committee that the natives were cowardly, the climate moderate, and the land good enough to support a large number of people and stock. He mentioned in passing that Botany Bay was some seven months' voyage from England. This point was not lost on the Government. When it did eventually decide to form a convict settlement at Botany Bay, one of the most telling, if least publicised, reasons was the distance of Botany Bay from England. The load of human garbage which the Government would project across the seas to the other side of the planet would find it difficult to float back and England would be a better place for that. As for Botany Bay, it would have to take its chances.

By January 20, 1788, the First Fleet had arrived in Botany Bay, under the command of Captain Arthur Phillip. On board the eleven ships were nineteen officers, twenty-four non-commissioned officers, eight drummers, one hundred and sixty privates, thirty wives and twelve children, and seven hundred and twenty-nine convicts. Such were the unlikely, and mostly unwilling, Pilgrim Fathers of white civilisation in Australia.

'Ithaca itself was scarcely more longed for by Ulysses, than Botany Bay by the adventurers who had traversed so many thousand miles to take possession of it,' wrote Captain Watkin Tench. Even the convicts might have momentarily shared Tench's enthusiasm; it had been a rough trip. But disenchantment with Botany Bay quickly set in, and nobody was more disenchanted than Phillip. His instructions were to proceed to the port called Botany Bay, 'the most eligible situation for the first establishment, possessing a commodious harbour and other advantages which no part of the coast hitherto discovered affords'.

Phillip swiftly concluded that Botany Bay afforded few advantages for his purpose. It was commodious but it was also shallow and exposed to easterlies while the shores were swampy and supplies of fresh water were insufficient for his needs.

While he landed men on the north side of the bay, he also quickly set to exploring, and

top: **Mangroves and wreckage**

middle: **Quibray Bay, Botany Bay**

above: **Sir Joseph Banks Hotel, Botany**

almost immediately discovered a harbour a few miles to the north which was ideally suited for a settlement. This harbour, Port Jackson, was deep and well sheltered, and a thousand ships of the line could ride there in perfect safety. Phillip decided to form at Port Jackson the settlement of Sydney, named for the Home Secretary, Lord Sydney, who had announced the decision to send convicts to New South Wales. One week after the First Fleet sailed into Botany Bay, it sailed out again.

Cook had spent a week in Botany Bay. Phillip did the same. Why were their impressions so different? Partly because their requirements were so different. Cook had wanted only shelter and refreshment for one small vessel for a short time. Phillip had to provide for the accommodation of great numbers and for ships of considerable burden to approach the shore and to lie in safety.

From Phillip's distinctly sarcastic comments on the matter, it appears that he laid the blame not on his fellow sea-captain, Cook, but on 'philosophical gentlemen', namely Joseph Banks. Time and distance and the recollection of his exciting botanical discoveries had lent enchantment to Banks' account of Botany Bay. Phillip dryly remarked: 'The appearance of the place is picturesque and pleasing, and the ample harvest it afforded, of botanical acquisitions, made it interesting to the philosophical gentlemen engaged in that expedition; but something more essential than beauty of appearance, and more necessary than philosophical riches, must be sought in a place where the permanent residence of multitudes is to be established.'

So Phillip dismissed Botany Bay from his mind and for some years to follow, while the infant colony at Sydney Cove struggled to establish itself and then to expand westward, Botany Bay was left to its own devices.

But in England, Ireland and Scotland, the name 'Botany Bay' was not so easily forgotten. Most people were illiterate and relied for their news and views on the 'broadsides', which were performed by street-balladeers, and which served the function then that popular daily papers serve now. The broadside-makers and their customers were keenly interested in all details of crime and punishment, and particularly in transportation. They were, after all, of the class that was most likely to be transported. When the possibility of a convict colony at Botany Bay was first discussed, the ballad-makers were quick to seize on the story. The first street-ballads about transportation to Botany Bay were circulating before a single convict had rattled his chains on Australian soil. The last song about Botany Bay was being sung in music-halls one century after Phillip had abandoned the place as useless.

The Botany Bay song that every Australian knows is the last one, which begins:

'Farewell to old England forever
Farewell to my rum culls as well
Farewell to the well-known Old Bailey
Where I used for to cut such a swell.

Singin' tooral li-ooral li-addity
Singin' tooral li-ooral li-ay
Singin' tooral li-ooral li-addity
And we're bound for Botany Bay.'

It is a jolly, rousing song which conveys little sense of Botany Bay as a destination of horror, but that is because the song was made long after the convict era ended. The earlier Botany Bay transportation ballads convey a quite different feeling. These verses are typical:

'Come all young men of learning, a warning take by me
I'll have you quit night walking and shun bad company
I'll have you quit night walking, or else you'll rue the day
And you will be transported and be sent to Botany Bay.

. . . To see my poor old father, as he stood at the bar
Likewise my dear old mother, her old grey locks she tore
And in tearing of her old grey locks these words to me did say
"O son! O son! What hast thou done, thou art bound for Botany Bay!"' '

There was also another type of Botany Bay broadside, written in a savage and vengeful strain by anonymous citizens who didn't propose to go to Botany Bay themselves, but knew a variety of coxcombs, fops, spongers and parasites who *should* be sent there:

'There's nightwalking strumpets who swarm in
each street
Proclaiming their calling to each man they meet,
They become such a pest that without more delay,
Those corrupters should be sent to Botany Bay.

There's monopolisers who add to their store
By cruel oppression and squeezing the poor,
There's butchers and farmers get rich in that way
But I'd have all such rogues sent to Botany Bay.

You lecherous whore-masters who practise vile arts
To ruin young virgins and break parents' hearts
Or from the fond husband the wife lead astray
Let such debauched stallions go to Botany Bay.

There's whores, pimps and bastards, a large costly
crew
Maintained by the sweat of the labouring few,
They should have no commission, place, pension or
pay
Such locusts should all go to Botany Bay.

The hulks and the jails have some thousands in
store
But out of the jails are ten thousand times more
Who live by fraud, cheating, vile tricks and foul
play
Should all be sent over to Botany Bay.'

above: **Sand dunes, Kurnell**

below: **Summer Sunday at Botany Bay**

Whatever else those verses might tell about the
condition of England in 1790, they leave no
doubt as to how Botany Bay was regarded. The
name, with its associations of exile, infamy and
despair, was branded into the consciousness of
the English, Irish and Scottish lower classes for
over half a century. (Funnily enough, if one
can derive any fun from an era as grim as the
convict period, the same sort of thing
happened in Australia in reverse. The
Cornstalks, the free-born sons and daughters of
convicts in New South Wales, when asked if
they felt any desire to visit England, replied,
'England? Gawd, no! That's where all the
convicts come from!')

Botany Bay, overseas, meant a place for
people that nobody wanted near them. What
in fact happened to Botany Bay in Australian
history was not quite that, but something
similar. The convict settlement was quickly
withdrawn, but after a relatively short period
of peace Botany Bay became a place for *things*
that nobody else wanted near them, and that
tradition has continued ever since.

It was, ironically, an ex-convict who started it. Simeon Lord, a man of tremendous energy and perseverance, developed the first industry at Botany in 1815, when he started a woollen mill there. Five years later, the members of the Philosophical Society of Australia resolved to commemorate the British discovery of Botany Bay. After some debate as to whether the brass tablet should be inscribed in English or Latin, they eventually drank their toasts to this inscription:

'UNDER THE AUSPICES OF BRITISH SCIENCE
THESE SHORES WERE DISCOVERED
BY
JAMES COOK & JOSEPH BANKS
THE COLUMBUS AND MAECENAS OF THEIR TIME
THIS SPOT ONCE SAW THEM IN THE PURSUIT OF KNOWLEDGE
NOW
TO THEIR MEMORY THIS TABLET IS INSCRIBED
IN THE FIRST YEAR
OF
THE PHILOSOPHICAL SOCIETY OF AUSTRALIA.'

If these philosophical gentlemen thought they were heralding a new vision of Botany Bay as a hallowed spot and the birthplace of a nation, they were badly mistaken. There were many types of noxious enterprises which Sydney felt it required. Sydney did not require such things at its front door, where they might offend the genteel noses that sniffed from the villas of Sydney Harbour. But it was content to have them at its back door.

Simeon Lord had pointed the way to Botany Bay, and other industrialists were quick to follow. The first wool washing mills were followed by tanneries, boiling-down works, blood and bone factories, soap and glue factories. Another doubtful acquisition was the Coast Hospital at Little Bay, a quarantine hospital for smallpox victims. Smallpox had arrived with the first white settlers in 1788. It soon buried most of the Botany Bay blacks, the Water People.

Phillip had abandoned Botany Bay partly because he thought the swamp water was unhealthy but it was precisely these stores of water that drew the milling and washing trades to Botany. In the same period, the Botany Swamp was the source of Sydney's fresh water supply. From 1859 onwards, the water was pumped up from the Swamp to hilltop reservoirs at Paddington and from there it was reticulated to the city. But in 1886 Sydney switched to the Nepean water supply. The Botany water had become unfit for drinking or domestic use. Sydney had the distinction of being the first Australian city to destroy its own water supply by gross industrial pollution.

That was nearly a century ago and since then the direction hasn't altered but the pace has quickened. Botany has now become the most industrialised area of Australia's most industrialised city. In the 1920s the adjoining area of Mascot was awarded Sydney Airport. Nowadays, proposals that it should be resited in some other area, such as Galston, can help to bring down governments.

The airport has had to expand to cope with the jet age and part of Botany Bay has been filled in to extend the runway. More has been filled in for breakwaters and container wharves — the bay has been awarded the honour of becoming Sydney's major container terminal, Port Botany. The harbour that Cook described as 'capacious' has been shrunk, or as some would say, reclaimed. The ghost of James Cook, if brought back to inspect his old anchorage now, would no doubt suffer a spectral coronary.

It would appear that old Botany Bay has become a ghost too and that there is nothing to be gained from lamenting the meadows and forests that were lost. Surprisingly though, there are still parts of the bay that remain as the first white men might have seen them. Over on the southern shores, in Quibray Bay, is the last remaining stand of mangroves in metropolitan Sydney. They are not mere decorations. Along with the salt marshes behind them and the sea grass on the floor of the bay the mangroves are vital to marine life. Mangroves are a rich source of food. One acre produces four tons of nutrient a year, which is equal to the value of one acre of rain forest, and ten times richer than one acre of wheat.

The delicate balance of this natural system in Botany Bay supports more than marine life; it supports human life. Botany Bay has had a long tradition as a fishing centre and there was for nearly 140 years a self-contained community called Fishing Town in the area of Booralie Street, Mascot. It numbered several hundreds and the same families lived and fished from there over five or six generations. Fishing Town has gone now, but Botany Bay still produces a rich marine harvest with a million dollars worth of fish and prawns a year and twenty million dollars worth of Sydney rock oysters. The workers in these industries, and the consumers of their products, have a case to be heard against the case of the container shippers. But some conservationists believe the fishing industry is already doomed in Botany Bay. The alteration of wave patterns by breakwaters and the dredging of the shallow bay to allow passage to huge tankers will, they say, destroy the sea grass-mangrove-dune system that supported marine life for thousands of years.

Also under threat from industrial development is Sydney's only haven and breeding ground for migratory wader birds, at Towra Point. There are sixty-six species of these birds and some thirty of these species have been sighted at Towra Point. They include the Eastern Curlew, the Bar-tailed Godwit, the Grey-tail Tattler — birds that migrate from Siberia, Alaska and Japan during the northern winters to summer at Botany Bay. It will be a sad thing not only for Australia, but for the world, if our actions at Botany Bay endanger these species.

Botany Bay has certainly been beset by industry since the early days of white settlement but industry is not its only tradition. It was also an early pleasure resort for the Sydney masses and the Sir Joseph Banks Hotel, built at Botany in 1842, was classed in its time as a pleasure dome par excellence. It advertised itself as 'a mecca for sportsmen, paradise for picnickers, happy hunting ground for all. No dangers, no delay, no overcrowding, no mal-de-mer'. There was a three-mile horse track and an athletic track that drew leading professional runners and punters. There was a cricket pitch, a bowling green, and an archery ground. Silvertails like Lord Carrington stayed at the hotel, politician Sir Henry Parkes drank there, the boxer Jack Johnson trained there in a special stadium.

Men could drink and gamble at the Sir Joseph Banks Hotel while the ladies strolled in the seaside grounds or gossiped in the summer houses — or, at least, that was the way it was expected to be. For grown-ups, there was dancing in the huge pavilion, and for children there was the Zoo. Formed in 1847, it was the first Zoo in the Colony and it included a Royal Bengal tiger, a Black Bear of the Himalayas, and an elephant which the children could ride.

The Sir Joseph Banks Hotel, having survived an attempt to demolish it, is still there, hidden away in a back street of Botany. It is now operated as a private guest house by Mrs Dorothy Ruttley, and few people know about it, but it stands as a visible reminder that Botany has seen other days and served other purposes than industry.

Many of the half a million people who live around the shores of Botany Bay still regard the bay as a natural asset, and a recreational place. Two thousand sailors belong to clubs in the district. On a summer Sunday, a thousand boats sail its waters for pleasure. Multitudes of people, speaking in every tongue, stroll its shores, bask on its beaches or fish from its banks. Pleasure, like history, is difficult to put a price tag on, but all these people have a claim on the use of the bay and who is to say their claim is less important than the industrial shippers' claim. Man does not live by tankers alone, though no doubt there are powerful interests prepared to swear that he does.

Botany Bay has a history of foreign invasion scares. Phillip got a dreadful fright, just as he was leaving the bay in 1788, when he sighted two strange ships outside the heads. He feared they were Dutchmen, come to dispute the British claims to New Holland. As it turned out, they were the ships of the French explorer, La Perouse, who was looking for a place to rest and make repairs. After a brief stay at Frenchman's Bay, La Perouse sailed away and was lost forever in the Pacific.

Almost a century later the colonials were gripped again by foreign invasion fever and they erected the fort that can still be inspected on Bare Island in Botany Bay. It was armed with five eighteen-ton muzzle-loading cannons, all pointed towards the Botany Bay Heads to ward off a supposed Russian invasion. But the Russians were not coming and the guns never fired a shot in anger. In any case, if they were meant to protect Botany Bay from attack, they were pointing the wrong way. The real threat to Botany Bay comes from us.

Another country might have preserved the whole area of their founding place as a national shrine. We have degraded Botany Bay and driven it down for over a century. What is lost now can't be brought back, and it would be unrealistic to suggest that it could. But there is still a point where we can stop the tunnel-visioned industrial over-development of the bay. There is still something there of our natural heritage and something of our historic heritage. If we can't save even a small piece of our past, perhaps we haven't much chance of saving our future.

top: **The shrinking Bay**

left: **The most industrialized area in Australia, Botany Bay**

opposite: **Wiseman's Ferry**

THE HAWKESBURY RIVER

Arthur Phillip, although he was the first Governor of New South Wales and one of its best Governors, is not usually classed amongst the great Australian explorers. But Phillip did quite well in the field of exploration. He moved the first settlement from Botany Bay to Sydney Cove in Port Jackson, and that was a good start.

Phillip, however, was uncomfortably aware that the colony would not survive long without finding better farming land than could be observed around Port Jackson. In March, 1788, two months after his arrival, he explored Broken Bay, the next bay north of Port Jackson, and found a large body of water extending back to the south towards Sydney. He named this Pitt Water, for the Prime Minister of England.

A year later he returned to Broken Bay, intent on finding a river which he thought should flow into the bay from the great mountain range that stood west of Sydney. He had named the northern part of this range the Carmathen Hills and the southern part the Lansdowne Hills but, because of the characteristic haze that covered the range, it was soon known as the Blue Mountains.

Phillip succeeded in finding the river — not too difficult a task as the river was indeed very large — and, with his party of sailors, he proceeded ninety miles upstream to a point where the major river was formed by the joining of two tributaries. Phillip and his party climbed the highest hill they could find in this area and Phillip named it Richmond Hill. The major river which he had ascended was called by the Aborigines Deerubbin. Phillip renamed it the Hawkesbury, for Lord Hawkesbury, the Head of the British Board of Trade.

It was not a particularly arduous or dangerous feat of exploration but it was a most useful and important discovery. The river, although comparatively short, was broad, beautiful, surrounded by fertile country and marvellously handy to Sydney. Some of Phillip's party ventured the opinion that, if Sydney had not already been founded, Richmond Hill might well have been the place for the chief settlement of the colony. Phillip himself reported to Lord Sydney:

'The breadth of this river (named the Hawkesbury) is from 300 to 800 feet; and it appears from the soundings we had to be navigable for the largest merchant ships to the foot of Richmond Hill; but as the water near the head of the river sometimes rises after very heavy rains thirty feet above its common level, it would not be safe for ships to go so far up; but fifteen or twenty miles below Richmond Hill they would lay in fresh water, and perfectly safe. I speak of Richmond Hill as being the head of the river, it there growing very shallow, and dividing into two branches.

'The high rocky country which forms Broken Bay is lost as you proceed up the Hawkesbury, and the banks of the river are there covered with timber, the soil a rich light mould; and, judging from the little we saw of the country, I should suppose it good land to a very considerable extent; the other branches of fresh water are shoal, but probably run many miles further into the country than we could trace them with our boats. On these rivers we saw great numbers of wild ducks, and some black swans; and on the banks of the Hawkesbury several decoys made by the natives for to catch the quail.

'Richmond Hill (near the foot of which a fall of water prevented our proceeding further with the boats) is the southern extremity of a range of hills, which, running to the northward, most probably join the mountains which lay nearly parallel to the coast, from fifty to sixty miles inland. The soil of Richmond Hill is good, and it lays well for cultivation. Our prospect from the hill was very extensive to the southward and eastward; the country appearing, from the height at which we were, to be a level covered with timber: there is a flat of six or seven miles between Richmond Hill and a break in the mountains, which separates Lansdowne and Carmathen Hills; and in this flat, I suppose, the Hawkesbury continues its course, but which could not be seen for the timber, that, with very few exceptions, covers the country wherever the soil is good.

'The great advantages of so noble a river, when a Settlement can be made on its banks, will be obvious to your Lordship.'

Phillip's verdict was just. The great advantages of this noble river were even more obvious to the colonists than they were to his Lordship in far-away London, and by 1794 several farmers were squatting on the banks of the Hawkesbury. In that year Grose made land grants on the Hawkesbury to twenty-two settlers and a year later there were some four hundred people in the district called Green Hills (later Windsor).

They rapidly felled the timber on the flats and sowed crops of wheat, barley and corn. Phillip, they discovered, had not underestimated the rich alluvial soil. It was capable of growing any crop in abundance. This was very good news in a colony that came perilously close to starvation in its early years and the Hawkesbury was soon on the way to establishing its reputation as the granary of the colony, 'the breadbasket of Sydney'.

But there was something else that Phillip *had* underestimated. During his trip up the river he had occasionally noticed debris hanging in trees high above the banks. In his report to Lord Sydney, he mentioned the possible risks to ships from the rise of the headwaters after rain. It did not occur to him to mention the possible risks to farmers. The Hawkesbury settlers quickly discovered that there was a catch to this noble river. What it gave so carelessly with one hand, it took away just as carelessly with the other. The alluvial soil that grew such marvellous crops was deposited by regular and prodigious floods, capable of sweeping away in a single night not only the settlers' yearly crops, but also their dwellings and their lives.

In March 1799, the settlers were warned by Aborigines of an impending flood, but they took as much notice of the Aborigines as they always did, namely, none whatever. The waters swept down at night, cutting off the families on the low ground and driving them into boats and rafts or on to their rooftops. Next morning, Green Hills looked like a sea, dotted with occasional islands and full of floating debris which included most of the farmers' crops and stock. Only one human life was lost but the river, risen fifty feet above normal level, had swept away the government storehouse and many of the settlers' crude dwellings.

Small floods were treated as commonplace on the Hawkesbury but big floods had a habit of arriving too often for comfort. In 1806,

another tremendous flood caused such damage that the Government ordered an investigation. It was found that 7 people, 16 horses, 47 sheep, 296 goats, 4 cattle and 3 563 pigs had been drowned; 24 000 bushels of wheat and 4 000 bushels of barley had been swept away; and 340 settlers, 454 labourers and convicts, 238 women and 461 children had suffered loss and damage from the flood. Whatever the Government investigation may have achieved, it didn't stop the floods, and another flood roared down the Hawkesbury in 1809.

One notable feature that emerged from these early Hawkesbury floods was the selfless courage shown by some of the settlers, who ventured out in their boats on the raging waters at night and effected quite remarkable rescues, sometimes saving upwards of one hundred people in a single night.

For most families it was a situation of stark terror and the official statistics do less to convey that terror than this account from the *Sydney Gazette:*

'The distress and horror of the evening can neither be described nor imagined — the day heavy and gloomy, the night fast approaching, torrents of rain pouring with unabating fury and not a house except at Green Hills to be seen, the roofs of one or two on the opposite side of the water being only then visible. Muskets were discharged by the settlers from trees and roofs all day; in the evening the distant cries from different quarters, the report of firearms dangerously charged in order to increase the noise of explosion, the howling of dogs that by swimming had got into trees, all combined to shock the feelings of the few that were out of reach, but were sorrowful spectators of the calamity they could not relieve. Among other wonderful escapes was that of William Leeson who with his mother, wife and two children and three men was carried from his farm upon a barley mow. They were driven 7 miles; were taken off in the dark by Richard Wallis with the greatest difficulty.'

In spite of these dreadful floods, a considerable community had settled on the Hawkesbury by 1809 and they had developed a distinct 'Hawkesbury spirit'. Most of them were ex-convicts or working-class free settlers, and their spirit was distinctly at odds with the spirit of Macarthur and the officers of the Rum Corps, particularly as they suspected those military gentlemen of rigging the Sydney market and cheating them of proper returns for their produce.

Governor Bligh was also no friend of the Rum Corps, but he liked the Hawkesbury settlers and they liked him. However, Bligh was deposed by the officers in the Rum Rebellion and in 1809 a new man, Lachlan Macquarie, was directed to go out and govern New South Wales. Amongst Macquarie's instructions, which were mostly to do with clearing up the debris of the Bligh affair, was an instruction that he should adopt precautionary measures to prevent the recurrence of famine occasioned by the inundations of the Hawkesbury.

Even Macquarie, a man who stood tall in the early history of Australia, particularly when compared to some of the mental and moral pigmies of the 'Exclusive' set, was not capable of preventing the inundations of the Hawkesbury. But a tour of the Green Hills district in 1810 convinced him that he could do something for the settlers and save their lives, if not their crops, by drawing them into market towns safely situated on high ground.

Accordingly, he invented his Five Towns. After preliminary surveys had been taken and the sites of the Five Towns fixed upon, Macquarie recorded in his journal on December 6, 1810:

'A large party of friends dined with us today, consisting in all of 21 persons, including our own family. After dinner I christened the new townships, drinking a bumper to the success of each. I gave the name of Windsor to the town intended to be erected in the district of the Green Hills, in continuation of the present village, from the

below: **The Hawkesbury — 'more enchanting than the Rhine'**

similarity of this situation to that of the same name in England; the township in the Richmond district I have named Richmond from its beautiful situation and as corresponding with that of its district; the township for the Evan or Nepean district I have named Castlereagh in honour of Lord Viscount Castlereagh; the township of the Nelson District I have named Pitt-Town in honour of the immortal memory of the late great William Pitt, the Minister who originally planned this Colony; and the township for the Phillip District, on the north or left bank of the Hawkesbury, I have named Wilberforce in honour of and out of respect to the good and virtuous Wm. Wilberforce Esqr. M.P. a true patriot and the real friend of mankind.'

right: **Classic Windsor**

below: **The heart of Colonial Hawkesbury**

One wonders how Castlereagh got on that list, in the company of 'real friends of mankind'. He was an arch-reactionary, to whom Shelley penned the immortal insult, in *The Mask of Anarchy:*

'I met Murder on the way—
He had a mask like Castlereagh.'

Byron described Castlereagh as a despot and an intellectual eunuch. Generally, he seems to have had all the warmth and humanity of an ice-cube. Macquarie honoured him, I would guess, because it was Castlereagh, as Secretary of State, who gave Macquarie his commission as Governor. There was a debt to repay.

In any case, the village named for Castlereagh was not destined for great things; nor were the villages named for those worthier gentlemen, Pitt and Wilberforce. Only two of the Five Towns grew to reflect Macquarie's great ambitions — Windsor and Richmond. In spite of the depredations of the twentieth century, both towns have retained many beautiful buildings from the early colonial period, and it is still possible to get from them a sense of what it must have been like to live in those times.

Windsor, in particular, still bears the stamp of Macquarie's vision of what a proper town should be. The Five Towns were intended to draw into them the settlers who were living in ramshackle huts on the flood-prone river flats. Therefore the towns should contain those things that farmers would want — market squares, stores, decent inns — as well as buildings of more noble purpose such as courthouses, schools and churches.

The lovely St Matthew's Church at Windsor is the most vivid realisation of Macquarie's dream. It is the landmark of the Windsor area, visible from many parts of the countryside, and it has been described as 'the heart of the colonial Hawkesbury'. It was built to Macquarie's direction on a site that he personally selected, but it was not raised to its present state of mellow magnificence before suffering a few mishaps along the way.

Macquarie himself laid the foundation stone of the church in 1817. He placed underneath the stone a holey dollar — which was a Spanish dollar with the centre punched out of it — and he made the brief speech, 'God prosper St Matthews!' Apparently, Macquarie reckoned without the irreligious spirits who lurked in the outer darkness of Windsor. It was thieves who prospered from this little ceremony. They came that night, raised the foundation stone, and stole the holey dollar. So Macquarie had to repeat the ceremony two days later. On this occasion he made a rather more pointed speech before depositing another holey dollar. But the thieves were in no way deterred by his criticism of their infamous deed, and they came again in the night and stole the second dollar.

Perhaps Macquarie could see this sequence of events being repeated forever or perhaps his Scottish instinct of thrift took over, but when he came to launch St Matthew's a third time he refrained from depositing a dollar under the foundation stone. Construction of the church proceeded, but not smoothly. Macquarie's convict architect, Francis Greenway, inspected the work and concluded that inferior mortar was being used. The building was pulled down again, right back to the foundations.

At this point, it must have seemed that there was some terrible hoodoo on St Matthew's Church. But all that had begun so ill ended well. The Church was rebuilt to a grander design, Greenway's own, and was completed as it stands now. Of all the many beautiful buildings in the Hawkesbury district, St Matthew's shines forth as the finest work of Australia's best colonial architect, and the best-preserved symbol of Lachlan Macquarie's impact on New South Wales.

That impact is more admired now than it was in the Governor's own time. In the churchyard of St Matthew's is a grave older than the church itself. It is the grave of Andrew Thompson. Like most of the Hawkesbury settlers, Thompson was an ex-convict. Transported at the age of seventeen for theft, he was pardoned in 1797 and came to Windsor when it was still called Green Hills.

Thompson, a man of tremendous enterprise, became the leading farmer and merchant of the district. His ships traded far and wide from Windsor. He built a granary, a brewery, a salt-works and a bridge across the Hawkesbury. Macquarie was so impressed by Thompson that he made him a Justice of the Peace and Chief Magistrate of the Hawkesbury.

The 'Pure Merinos', the exclusive set in the colony, were aghast that Macquarie should lay such honours on an ex-convict. These were the men who clung to the notion of 'Botany Bay', a permanent prison camp where squires and parsons would be squires and parsons forever, and convicts would be convicts forever, supplying their cheap labour to squires and parsons for as long as the flogger and the hangman spared their contemptible lives. These exclusive worthies made things as hot as they could for Macquarie. But the Governor was unabashed. He had a different vision of the future, a vision of 'Australia' (a name he made official in 1817), a new country where a man's chances would depend on what he did in it, not on what he might have done, years ago, on the other side of the world.

So Macquarie ignored the bleating of the Pure Merinos and when the ex-convict Thompson died in 1810 (worn out, it was said, by his exertions in saving over a hundred people in the Hawkesbury flood), it was Macquarie who wrote the epitaph that can still be read in St Matthew's churchyard. In it he described Thompson as a most valuable and useful man and the principal founder of Windsor.

Macquarie didn't stop there. In his diary of January 12, 1811, he recorded:

'The Square in the present town I have named Thompson Square in the honour of the memory of the good and worthy late Andrew Thompson Esquire, Justice of the Peace and Principal Magistrate for this district and who may be justly said to be the father and founder of the village hitherto known as Green Hills.'

Thompson Square is still there, a reminder of the achievements of Andrew Thompson and the determination of Lachlan Macquarie to honour him for them. Some things have gone — the old stocks and the convict flogging post, and Thompson's own house, which overlooked the square and commanded a grandstand view of the floggings, a situation which may have forcibly intruded on Andrew Thompson unwelcome memories of his own earlier days. The square is still the historic centre of Windsor,

and there are buildings around it that tell the story of the town as it marched through the nineteenth century. The earliest, the Macquarie Arms, is another of those buildings directly commissioned by the Governor himself. On January 12, 1811, he stated in his journal:

'I gave Mr Fitzgerald a large allotment in the Square on the express condition of his building immediately thereon a handsome commodious Inn of brick or stone and to be at least two stories high.'

Mr Fitzgerald's building activities were not strikingly immediate — it was not till 1815 that Macquarie returned to formally open the establishment — but he did build a handsome and commodious inn, which is now claimed to be the oldest building erected as an inn in Australia.

On the wall — a wall made of bricks that were rejected for St Matthew's Church — is a reminder that the river, unlike the hills of Windsor, refused to be domesticated. The wall indicates the high water mark of the Great Flood of 1867, the worst in the history of the Hawkesbury. To the present day, the Hawkesbury has not stopped flooding. Since 1799, one hundred and sixty floods have been recorded — almost one a year. Fifty of them are classed as major floods. The damage done, in loss of homes and stock and crops, runs into untold millions of dollars.

Life has not changed greatly for the modern Hawkesbury farmers. Some of them believe that the flooding has become worse in the last thirty years than it ever was before. Various reasons are suggested — changes in weather patterns, the Warragamba Dam, or bulldozing of timber in the catchment area which has increased the run-off of mountain waters into an increasingly silted river. Actually, the silting of the river seems to have started a long time ago, perhaps as early as the first clearing of timber. Ships of considerable size sailed right up to Windsor wharf in the early nineteenth century, but by the end of the century, the river had become too shallow to allow it. Eventually, the freighter boats that had once carried the farmers' fruit and crops to market died out completely, but from a different cause — competition from motor transport.

Whatever causes the floods, the warier farmers still make sure they build their houses on high ground as their ancestors learned to do in Macquarie's time. The crops are different now. Wheat is not grown; the main lines are citrus or vegetables for the Sydney market. But such crops are still regularly wiped out by floods and a number of farmers have turned to growing turf, which can survive flooding. The turf is sliced off when ready, rolled up and sold in Sydney as instant lawn.

One unusual crop, grown in the Hawkesbury district a century ago, was wine-grapes. The man responsible for this was a Dr Thomas Fiaschi, who, from 1879 to 1883, occupied the charming old building on the river corner of Thompson Square, Windsor, which is called the Doctor's House.

below: **Andrew Thompson's grave at St Matthew's Church, Windsor**

below right: **Peter Auld at the Tizzana Winery**

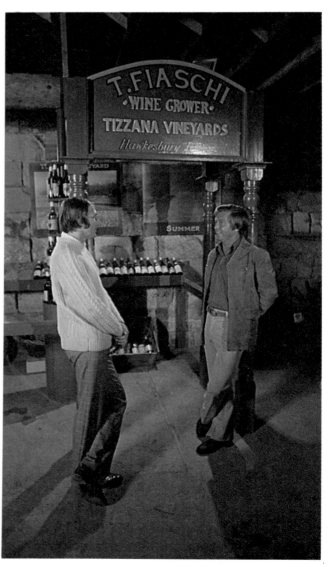

left: Wiseman's Ferry Inn

below: The oldest ferry in Australia, Wiseman's Ferry

Dr Fiaschi was quite an exceptional character. He was born in Florence, graduated from the Universities of Florence and Pisa, migrated to Cooktown in Queensland and from there to Windsor. After some years of doctoring in Windsor he became a distinguished surgeon at Sydney Hospital and later rose to high rank in both the Australian and Italian armies. He was awarded numerous decorations for bravery and devotion to duty. He was also a literary man, and was president of the Dante Alighieri Society in Sydney when he died in 1927.

But his first love was viticulture, and while he was at Windsor, he founded the Tizzana Winery, down river at Sackville Reach. He had 55 acres under grapes, was keenly interested in the product of the vine, and tried to interest other people in a period when wine was not the fashionable tipple it is now.

In fact Fiaschi was frowned on in some quarters because he advocated the use of wine as medicine and prescribed it in generous quantities to his patients. Some felt that he was getting his twin professions of doctor and vigneron mixed up, but Fiaschi stoutly asserted that wine, in most cases, improved both the health and the disposition of his patients. He insisted that nurses should serve wine to his patients, not from medicine bottles, but from proper wine bottles and in the correct glasses, and he wrote learned treatises as to which conditions could best be treated by prescriptions of hock, port and so on. One patient, to whom he had prescribed champagne, asked how often she should dose herself. Fiaschi replied: 'As often as your pocket can stand it.' The impish old doctor would be pleased to know that his beautiful stone winery at Tizzana has been restored and is once again selling wine.

The history of the Hawkesbury settlement proceeded like the Hawkesbury itself, beginning at the head of the river around Richmond, Windsor and smaller settlements like Ebenezer, at Portland Head, where Australia's oldest church still stands, and where the last traditional river funeral, a procession of boats with muffled oars, was held for John Grono in 1917.

Further downriver, where the farming land diminished and the broad Hawkesbury flowed between high sandstone cliffs, settlement was slower to commence. One of the few early settlers along the middle stretch of the river was Solomon Wiseman. Solomon knew something about rivers; he had been a Thames waterman and was transported for stealing a cargo of timber on the Thames. In New South Wales he managed to restore his fortunes and when he came to the Hawkesbury he selected one of its prettiest places, about midway on the river between Richmond Hill and Broken Bay. Solomon built here his mansion-cum-inn, Cobham Hall, and also operated a ferry service for stock and the occasional traveller.

In 1830 he had a great stroke of good fortune when Wiseman's Ferry was selected as the crossing place for the Great North Road which Governor Darling decreed should be built from Sydney to the Hunter River (or Coal River as it was originally called). An establishment of seven hundred convicts was set to work to build the road, working in irons under military guard and living in boxes on wheels, sixteen men to a box.

Solomon Wiseman made a fortune selling meat and grog to this road-building outfit while his ferry became so busy that he was soon able to sell it to the Government at a handsome profit. A century and a half later it's still operating, the oldest ferry service in Australia.

Wiseman's old house, Cobham Hall, is part of the present Wiseman's Ferry Inn and is rumoured to be vigorously haunted by at least three resident ghosts. One is a convict servant that Solomon Wiseman allegedly had flogged to death. The second is his wife, Jane, whom Solomon is supposed to have hurled from the upstairs balcony down on to the front steps. On moonlit nights, the legend has it, blood stains appear on these steps and the ghost of Jane Wiseman haunts the scene, wearing a long nightdress and a gloomy expression. (Actually Jane Wiseman could not have been dashed down on the steps, as she died of an illness in 1821, five years before Cobham Hall was built.) The third ghost is that of Solomon himself. When he died the old lag was buried in full ceremonial dress, with a frock coat, boots, a sword, a diamond ring and a gold watch. The temptation was too much for the local vandals who desecrated Wiseman's grave.

According to Hawkesbury legend, it wasn't only the valuables that disappeared from the grave; local fishermen souvenired the lead from the coffin to hang as weights on their nets, while the bones were scattered and the skull was kicked around the river flat as a football. Eventually, old Solomon's bones were got together again and reburied in a churchyard, but perhaps his ghost haunts the inn hoping to revenge the indignities done to his first grave.

The traces of the convicts who built the Great North Road can still be seen at Wiseman's Ferry. South of the river convict-cut steps still lead to an overhanging ledge called Judgment Rock where convicts from the road gang were hauled up to be tried for misdemeanours. Some of them were despatched on a last trip over the river to Hangman's Rock, up where the traces of the Great North Road still wind away into the bush. Despite all that convict blood and sweat and despite their massive job of constructing in stone a monument to the penal era which can still be inspected north of Wiseman's Ferry, the Great North Road is no longer in use. Travellers to Newcastle and the Hunter River now cross the Hawkesbury lower down at Brooklyn.

It was at Brooklyn that one could say the industrial age came to the Hawkesbury with the construction of the first Hawkesbury River Railway Bridge in 1889. Fortunately, both for the river people and for the three million people of Sydney who now value the Hawkesbury as a prime recreational resort, the industrial age steamed and later motored over its bridges without descending on the river itself.

Brooklyn still holds a key position on the river. For touring motorists on National Route One, it is the place where they meet the Hawkesbury. For rail travellers, it is the Hawkesbury River Station and fast electric trains have put it right on the commuter run. The former river port is on the way to becoming a Sydney suburb and the river itself is practically a second Sydney Harbour, but a harbour for pleasure rather than profit.

The Hawkesbury has a long history as a sporting venue. Perhaps its most curious event took place in 1845 when a rolling race through deep mud was staged on its banks between two gentlemen named Kurrajong Sawyer and Mad Arthur. It was always a favoured spot for picnics, fishing and regattas, and it has produced some outstanding athletes. The world champion sculler, Peter Kemp, learned to row on the Hawkesbury, and Boy Charlton swam some of his early races there.

Since 1934, it has been the venue of one of the world's speedboat classics, the Bridge to Bridge race from Brooklyn to Windsor, and in recent years it has become a mecca for waterskiers. There is some conflict between the adherents of these newer and noisier sports and those who wish to use the river for more tranquil pursuits. The Hawkesbury's big problem is the proximity of a huge city, and the numbers of people who want to use it for different things, which are not all compatible with each other.

There are also threats to the quality of the Hawkesbury from the gravel-extraction industry in its upper reaches and from proposals to empty more of Sydney's sewage into its tributaries. But it does not have problems that are drastic, irreversible, or beyond human ingenuity to solve. Unlike that other 'second Sydney Harbour', Botany Bay, the Hawkesbury does not induce feelings of despair. It still has a tremendous amount to offer in history, in beauty and in simple pleasure for the people who cruise its waters.

Amongst the many picturesquely named stretches of the Hawkesbury, such as Sentry-Box Reach and Milkmaid's Reach, there is one called Trollope Reach. This was not, as its name might suggest, a marine beat for river harlots. It was named for the English author, Anthony Trollope, who cruised the Hawkesbury a century ago and declared it superior to both the Rhine and the Mississippi. 'The Hawkesbury,' he wrote, 'has neither castles nor islands, nor has it bright clear water like the Rhine. But the headlands are higher, the bluffs are bolder, and the course the water has made is grander, and to me more enchanting, than those of either the European or the American river.'

31

Provided that a Hawkesbury River Authority is set up to control the whole river, prevent over-development and stop the processes that have turned the once 'bright clear water of the Rhine' into liquid industrial waste, Trollope's words should remain true for centuries to come. So should the prophecy of Governor Phillip, that this noble river would prove to be of great advantage to the country.

left: **Australia's living past**

below left: **Judgement Rock, Wiseman's Ferry**

below: **Cabbage fields at Cornwallis, Upper Hawkesbury**

opposite: **Abandoned tunnel, Maryvale — Sandy Hollow Railway**

FOLLIES

Governor Macquarie's vision of the future Australia went much further than the creation of the Five Towns. His aim was to give the whole colony what he felt it most needed — a sense of self-respect and of hope — and to make it the sort of place where men of intelligence, education and enterprise could settle without misgivings and backward glances at the Europe they had left.

During his eleven years in New South Wales he went quite a way towards achieving his aim, and after he had returned to London he wrote to Earl Bathurst in 1822 and offered this verdict on his own achievements:

'I found the colony barely emerging from infantile imbecility, and suffering from various privations and disabilities; the Country impenetrable beyond forty miles from Sydney . . . the few Roads and Bridges, formerly constructed, rendered almost impassable . . .

'I left it . . . reaping incalculable advantages from my extensive and important discoveries in all directions . . . This change may indeed be ascribed in part to the natural operation of time and events on individual enterprize: How far it may be attributed to measures originating with myself, . . . and my zeal and judgment in giving effect to my instructions, I humbly submit to His Majesty and his Ministers.'

It may be seen from this letter that Macquarie was not a modest man. But then he had no call to be. He had come to New South Wales with instructions from King George to build roads and plan townships but everything that he achieved was at the cost of constant niggling, criticism and reprimands from the Colonial Office in London.

Macquarie's energy and imagination were insufficient to make the colony grow. It was also necessary to spend money. Every time he spent some money, the Colonial Office demanded to know where all this money was going, and why. A lesser man might have pulled his horns in, but Macquarie was determined to give the colony a new shape (or, as his critics put it, to make the colony his own monument). He was particularly concerned with the colony's chief township, Sydney.

At the time Macquarie first saw it, Sydney had just reached the age of twenty-one but it was far from being a grown-up city. Rather, it had grown out in a haphazard and formless way from that first tiny settlement at Sydney Cove. Macquarie decided that this was not good enough. If Sydney Town were ever to become a city and the capital of an important society in some future time, it must have a proper plan, wide and well-formed streets and noble public buildings to impress the eyes and uplift the spirits of its citizens.

With the aid of his architect, Francis Greenway, Macquarie set out to create the foundations of such a city. If the Home Government had not stepped in there is no telling how far this pair might have gone. Sydney today would certainly wear a different face (if we can assume that the city Macquarie and Greenway planned to create would not have been totally destroyed again by the vandals of later generations). But in 1819 the British Government, aghast at the bills that were being presented from a place they had hoped would operate as a self-financing and satisfactorily remote gaol, sent Commissioner Bigge to Sydney. Bigge's mission was to find out where all the money was going, and to cut expenses back to the bone. His instructions, and his instincts, were against the spirit of everything Macquarie was trying to do. Macquarie was in the process of creating a Georgian capital for a new country. Bigge could only see Sydney as the base settlement for a penal colony. What would such a place want with grand courthouses or ambitious schools or churches? The only public buildings of any scale that Bigge could conceive of as necessary for Sydney were new gaols. Even so early in the history of the complex relations between Britain and Australia there was also in Bigge's attitude a certain element of keeping the colonials in their place. He rather gave the game away when he said, in shocked tones, of Greenway: 'If this fellow is suffered to go on, he will build a city superior in architecture to London!' That, of course, would never have done. Sydney had not been founded to outshine London. It had been founded as a repository for the scum of British prisons. One thought, that the Australian experience of the colonists might have changed their ideas of what was possible and desirable in this new country, did not trouble Bigge's mind. He was here with a job to do and he intended to get it over with.

Bigge had no trouble in finding kindred spirits in the colony. The wealthy snobs loathed Macquarie for his sympathetic treatment of ex-convicts. They also regarded his expenditure on public buildings as a waste of money. They regarded all public expenditure as a waste of money with the exception of funds spent to maintain the roads to their properties and to maintain the endless flow of cheap convict labour that was making their private fortunes.

These allies were quick to point out to Bigge one prime current example of Macquarie's madness: the Governor had conceived a scheme for a grand Government House in the Gothic style, to be modelled on Thornbury Castle in Gloucestershire. He had commissioned Greenway to build it and Greenway had gone even further and produced a landscaping scheme for the whole of Sydney Harbour. The islands and even the furthest headlands were to be dotted with castles and other features, in the manner of the English landscaper, Capability Brown. Fortunately, they told Bigge, the scheme had not yet proceeded so far. But a building in the process of construction at the foot of Macquarie Street would illustrate what they had said. It was a large building, an ornate building, an expensive building. It was spoken of as a mad extravagant folly, the butt and jest of every foreigner. And this, Bigge was informed, was not even to be the new Government House. This was merely to be the *stables!* That was all Bigge needed to know.

Not long after Bigge's visit, Macquarie left Australia and his Sydney Harbour scheme vanished into the limbo of forgotten Sydney plans. The stables, designed to house the Governor's thirty horses, his coaches and livery servants, were completed by Greenway and in later years became the Conservatorium of Music — perhaps the only Conservatorium of Music in the world to be housed in a stable. The central courtyard has been roofed in and the building considerably altered and extended but the western facade, facing Macquarie Street, still appears as Greenway intended.

Was the grand scheme, in which the stables were just the first step, a 'mad, extravagant folly'? A dictionary definition of 'folly', in the architectural sense, is 'a useless but costly structure often in the form of a sham Gothic or classical ruin, especially popular in eighteenth century England'. It may be that the scheme, if completed, might have come near to this definition. It was certainly Gothic. This was not Greenway's normal style but Macquarie had a fancy for Gothic. However, although Greenway's plans for the distant islands and headlands were left hazy I doubt if he intended to decorate them with sham ruins.

In any case, in this chapter I am not writing of 'follies' in the architectural sense but rather in the sense of schemes that never came to fruition. Macquarie's Sydney Harbour project certainly meets that definition and so do hundreds of others. Australia's history and Australia's landscape are littered with dreams that failed and grand schemes that somehow went off the rails. Some were grander than others, some were more foolish than others, but they all went wrong.

To take another Gothic example, there is a structure, just a few miles north of the site where Macquarie wanted his Government House castle, that looks from certain angles like the answer to his dream. It has turrets of masonry, castle battlements, towers with gun emplacements for one hundred and twelve mock cannon. Shift your angle of vision slightly, and the structure is revealed as a bridge. It is one of Sydney's most surprising and least noticed bridges, the Suspension Bridge between the suburbs of Northbridge and Cammeray. The thousands of motorists who drive over this bridge each day would be surprised and puzzled to hear that the Northbridge Suspension Bridge was a failure. But it was, for the men who built it.

This striking bridge was the brainchild of a syndicate of land-speculators called 'The North Sydney Tramway and Investment Company'. They built the bridge in 1891 at the frightening cost, for that day, of 100 000 pounds. Why the company chose such an

elaborate and expensive bridge design is not clear, but the purpose of the bridge was to carry tramloads of landbuyers over to the estate that the company was subdividing at Northbridge. Unfortunately for the speculators, they were a little premature. The tramline that was to carry the eager buyers over the bridge didn't arrive from North Sydney for another twenty years, and without the expected flood of buyers the North Sydney Tramway and Investment Company went broke. Even the desperate measure of charging every pedestrian threepence to walk over the bridge didn't generate enough income to save the company. The bridge was taken over in 1912 by the New South Wales Government.

left: **Governor Macquarie**

below: **Conservatorium of Music**

When it was first opened the bridge was proudly compared with America's most famous suspension bridge, the Brooklyn Bridge. The cables were replaced by an arch and girders in 1936 but the bridge is still popularly known as the Suspension Bridge. It certainly kept the North Sydney Tramway and Investment Company in suspense until they went bust. Nowadays it operates as a useful traffic link, even though it ruined the men who built it. They had suffered the misfortune of having an idea that was ahead of its time.

In the upper Hunter Valley can be found the remains of a vastly more ambitious transport link, the Maryvale-Sandy Hollow railway line. It was also an idea ahead of its

right: **Sandy Hollow Railway Station**

below: **Suspension Bridge, Northbridge**

time when it was first proposed nearly a century ago, but rising costs and diminishing freight prospects over the long years eventually made it an idea that was long past its time, and it was abandoned. Not, however, before $5 000 000 had been spent on the scheme. The Maryvale-Sandy Hollow line was to become the most expensive railway that Australia ever failed to build.

The idea, which was first put up in the 1880s, was to link the Macquarie River Valley and the Hunter River Valley settlements by railway. This would not only aid decentralisation and closer settlement but it would provide the western farmers with an alternative port. The port of Sydney was already becoming choked up and this new line would enable the farmers to rail their wheat and wool to Newcastle or to a new port to be built at Port Stephens. The people of Port Stephens, a lovely holiday haven just north of Newcastle, are probably happy now that the line never arrived. However, if it had been commenced in the 1880s, the great age of Australian railway construction, it's highly probable that the line would have been completed and would be in use today.

The problem, as usual, was money. Other schemes were given higher priority, and nothing was done about the Maryvale-Sandy Hollow line for thirty years. Then in 1913 a Royal Commission, after enquiring into the matter, recommended that the line should be built.

New South Wales politicians could not be accused of rushing headlong into a decision about the line. It was not until 1927 that the Government passed an act to build the line. The Government immediately lost interest again and it was not until the middle of the 1930s that work actually began. And then it was for political reasons rather than economic reasons. It was seen as a useful way of employing men thrown out of work by the Depression. Nevertheless, the line was at least begun. It was intended to run 125 miles, from Maryvale on the Western line near Wellington, to Sandy Hollow on the eastern side of the Great Dividing Range. A spur line already existed between Sandy Hollow and Muswellbrook, which was on the main Northern line.

Thus, the main Western line was to be linked with the main Northern line. Wheat and wool from as far west as the railhead at Bourke, on the Darling, could be shipped east to the port on the Hunter, Newcastle, or north to Brisbane. (No further mention was made of Port Stephens.) And all the goods required by the west could be railed back the same way.

Great capital was made of the benefits this would bring to the people of the inland. The fact that the main Northern and main Western railway lines had already been linked by a line built in 1924 from Dubbo through Binnaway to Werris Creek seems to have escaped everyone except the Railway Commissioners. They believed that the Binnaway line was capable of carrying all the freight available and that the Maryvale-Sandy Hollow line could only run at a loss.

Despite the opposition of the Railway Commissioners, work proceeded on the Maryvale-Sandy Hollow line for fourteen years from 1936. Little more than maintenance work was done during World War Two, but during the periods of construction more than four hundred men were employed on the line. They had quite a job in front of them. The line demanded five tunnels (one of them to be the longest in New South Wales), sixteen major bridges and thirteen stations and all this to be constructed in very rough and inaccessible country. The proponents of the line claimed that this route would give far easier grades than the Blue Mountains line — one in eighty as against one in thirty — and would therefore run longer and heavier trains, run them faster and so save money.

However, by 1950 the New South Wales Government decided that the best way it could save money was by cutting its losses and suspending work on the line. The Maryvale-Sandy Hollow railway was never officially abandoned but once work stopped, it never started again. The irony was that by this time the railway could have been finished. It might have run at a loss, but at least it would have run and brought benefit to somebody. Four of the five great tunnels were bored, and only half a mile remained to be bored in the No. 3 Tunnel. Most of the earthworks were completed, the pylons were being built for the bridges, some station platforms were in place. There was, perhaps, two years' work left and it could have been done for six million dollars.

But a quarter of a century's inflation has intervened and to complete the line now would cost $40 000 000. Local progress associations from the district, who still agitate politicians to get the line restarted, have a forlorn hope. They quoted, in one of their recent submissions, Einstein's remark 'Imagination is more important than knowledge'. Certainly Einstein cared strongly for imaginative vision but he was also handy at sums, and I think he might have felt that $40 000 000 was a relatively large sum to pay to bring this particular vision to reality.

As it remains, the Maryvale-Sandy Hollow line is a folly — costly and practically useless. One of its tunnels is used by cars on a minor road. Others are sporadically used for growing mushrooms but, at $5 000 000, they'd have to be classed as the most expensive mushroom farms in the world.

The Minister for Transport, Mr Bruxner, stated in 1937: 'This is the most important railway line remaining unfinished in the State.' If he'd said 'expensive' instead of 'important', then he'd have made one of those rare political statements that remain irrefutably true forty years after being uttered.

All the workers ever got out of the Maryvale-Sandy Hollow railway were some bitter-sweet memories — blistered hands from eight hours a day on the shovel, or banjo, for the princely sum of £7/17/6 a fortnight; tent camps along the line and rough and ready bush entertainments where the favourite tipple was Krantz's wine. It was a shilling a bottle and it was called 'Hen Wine' because, as they said at the time, 'You lay where you drank it.'

All the farmers ever got out of the line was a rousing ballad, penned by local optimists, about how tremendous it was going to be when the trains came:

'And we'll all give a cheer, on that wonderful day
When we've finished that old railway line.'

Farmers have to be optimists in Australia. As they often put it themselves: 'You don't have to be crazy, but it helps.' Nevertheless, this spirit of unquenchable optimism has sometimes led to tragedy, particularly in the earlier days of the country when there was an inability to recognise that European methods of farming didn't fit the climate and conditions of Australia.

Monuments to this particular brand of folly can be seen in the mid-north of South Australia, below the Flinders Ranges, where all that remains of a once-prosperous farming community is a scattering of ghost towns, and the rusting skeletons of agricultural machinery slowly falling apart in paddocks. Within thirty years of the foundation of South Australia, most of the best farming land in the south had been taken up, and there was pressure on the Government to throw open the land further north for farming. But the Government was warned by G. W. Goyder that to do this would be to risk disaster.

Goyder, who was for many years the Surveyor-General of South Australia, was one

above: G. W. Goyder, 'Little Energy'

39

of the remarkable men of Australian history. He was nick-named 'Little Energy'; not because he lacked energy — he had that in abundance — but because he was little, about five feet tall, with gingery hair. He was an acute observer and a straightforward man who said what he believed to be true, rather than what others wanted to hear. In 1865, during a severe drought, he surveyed the country to the north and came back with a line drawn on the map of South Australia. It ran up the eastern side of Spencer's Gulf, looped through the Southern Flinders Ranges and then down again to the south-east, passing near the town of Burra and extending over towards Swan Reach on the Murray River. This line, he said, was the limit of useful rainfall for agriculture. Outside the line, farming could not be permanently sustained. Goyder was very definite about the matter. He said that he'd seen vegetation on one side of the line, bare earth on the other side.

below: **The pub of J. J. O'Dea, 'The Baron of Yatina'**

Goyder's Line, as it became known, was a subject of tremendous contention. Goyder, who was in fact an incorruptible public servant, was accused of drawing up a line to protect the pastoralists who ran their flocks in the north, and to keep farmers out of perfectly good country. Goyder's Line was spoken of as if it were not an exact piece of observation and surveying, but a fanciful whim. Motions were put in Parliament to have Goyder's Line shifted further north and even to have it pushed right out of South Australia.

The Government eventually buckled under the pressure of expanding population and opened up the country beyond Goyder's Line for farming. A wave of would-be wheat cockies surged to the north and by the time they'd finished picking over the land some had settled a hundred miles beyond Goyder's Line.

There followed several years of good rains and the northern plains were golden with wheat. Bags of wheat were stacked like mountains beside the railway line to be carried away to Port Augusta, Port Pirie and Port

Wakefield, and from there shipped overseas. South Australia was earning more money from wheat than any other colony in Australia and much of it was coming from the area they christened 'The Golden North'.

It appeared that Goyder's Line was a fraud. Goyder had forgotten, the farmers said, an old piece of agricultural wisdom which they had imported to this new country. Rain followed the plough. Breaking the land open to sow crops released the moisture from the earth and this evaporated to form clouds. These clouds attracted other clouds and thus cultivation increased rainfall. So they thought.

The farmers had not really understood what Goyder was saying. He had never claimed that copious annual rains would fall one inch inside his magic line and that no rain would ever fall one inch outside it. Instead, he was talking about something that a colony that was keen

right: **'The Heartbreak Plains'**

below: **Machinery abandoned to the elements**

on horse-racing should have understood — the odds. From his observation of the vegetation, he forecast that permanent farming was likely to succeed inside his line and likely to fail outside it. The further inside the line, the better the odds; the further outside the line, the worse the odds.

The 1880 season dawned well, but there were no follow-up rains and the wheat crop failed. The next two years were worse. By 1883, many of the farmers were facing ruin. The Government offered them the option of giving up their selections and moving further south, but surprisingly few got out at once. They had staked their all on pioneering this country and they weren't going to give up without a struggle. Some struggled on in abject poverty till the end of their lives, waiting like parched Micawbers for something to turn up. Others eventually gave up and walked off. The land they had once called 'The Golden North' they now called 'The Heartbreak Plains'. Dreams and schemes of independence on their own farms had vanished. Goyder had told them something they didn't wish to know, but he had told the truth. Wishful thinking could not beat or alter the nature of this country, as the would-be cockies discovered the hard way.

The planners in Adelaide had envisaged an orderly farming community in the north — farms of one square mile, a market town every ten miles. Nowadays, those ridiculously small holdings have been incorporated back into the large grazing properties. Many of the towns have vanished completely. Others like Hammond, once a town of six hundred people with three big stores and an agricultural machinery factory, survive as tiny outposts for a handful of people too stubborn to leave. Their mellow stone buildings crumble away in the golden Northern sunlight; their streets are silent except for the flapping of corrugated iron peeling from desolate roofs.

The most telling monument to that age of terrific optimism, when men thought that the whole country was just waiting there to be conquered, is Yatina. It consists now of a post office and a delicensed pub, owned by a genial man named J. J. O'Dea. J. J. is called 'The Baron of Yatina' because he owns practically everything there, such as it is. But had Yatina proceeded according to plan, it would have been South Australia's biggest township outside Adelaide. Its streets, public buildings, parks and squares would have covered four square miles. Of course, Yatina didn't proceed to plan. The plan itself was a folly, drawn up by men who were too far from the scene.

This was the type of folly that recurred most often in Australian history. The plans weren't necessarily stupid in themselves; some were quite admirable. They just didn't fit the nature of the country. There seemed to be a reluctance to admit that Australia was a different country with its own set of rules. Indeed, the less the planners knew about the country, the further away they were from the actual scene, the grander were the schemes they drew up.

Perhaps the grandest of all these schemes was Australind. This dream city of a thousand acres, surrounded by one hundred thousand acres of closely settled farms, was to be founded on the Brunswick River in Western Australia, a hundred miles south of Perth and just north of the present-day site of Bunbury.

Australind was the brainchild of the Western Australian Company, a wealthy concern formed in London in 1839. The gentlemen involved were greatly impressed by the apparent success of the South Australian colony and one of the directors was Edward Gibbon Wakefield. The Western Australian Company proposed to follow Wakefield's system of planned emigration, and transfer an English society of squires, tenant farmers and agricultural labourers to Australian soil. Profits from the sale of land at Australind were to finance a continuing flow of emigrants to the colony and also provide a healthy return to the Company.

Apart from profit, the Company's choice of Australind was influenced by another consideration which it mentioned in its prospectus, issued from 6 Adelphi Terrace, The Strand, London in July 1840, 'namely, its great distance from the Convict Settlements, and the consequently superior social condition which already exists in Western Australia where the strongest repugnance to the convict system has prevailed.' (Western Australia was to become a convict colony twenty-eight years later, because it was going backwards as a free settlement, but the Company's directors could hardly be blamed for not foreseeing that.)

The Western Australian Company initially had no trouble in raising money from English subscribers and the ship *Island Queen* was chartered to take a surveying establishment to Australind. Marshall Waller Clifton, an English civil servant who had been chosen as Chief Commissioner of the Company, was to follow shortly afterwards with 'a powerful body of colonists'.

At a farewell luncheon to the surveyors at Lovegrove's West India Dock Tavern on August 31, 1840, Waller Clifton said:

'As an *Australindian* I speak and express the hope that at no distant period I may see the new settlement take an important station among the Colonies of the British Empire, and Australind as the maritime capital of Western Australia, not only the emporium of trade and commerce, but distinguished for its high moral, religious and intellectual character.'

The extraordinary ambitions expressed in this speech were also reflected in a map produced by the Company, which showed Australind at the centre of the world, with every important maritime route leading to it. The name Australind, a combination of Australia and India, was another expression of this notion that had somehow become fixed in the Company's mind — that their settlement was ideally situated on the trade routes between Europe and the East, and destined to become a great maritime centre, an Australian Singapore.

The Western Australian Company may have known nothing about Australia, but they knew what they wanted and the plan for the intended town of Australind, which was produced by Waller Clifton and his surveyors, spelled it out. On the shores of Leschenault Inlet and along the Brunswick River a great city was to rise — a city of churches, colleges, hospitals, quays, parklands, broad streets and noble squares, such as Victoria Square and Prince Albert Square; a city something like London at its best. There would be 20 000

citizens, which was more than Perth had, but then Australind was expected to supplant Perth and become the new capital.

This glorious scheme was wrecked almost at the moment it began. A doubt arose as to whether the Company had a proper title to the land they'd bought at Leschenault Inlet. Simultaneously, the explorer George Grey, arriving home from Western Australia, announced that Leschenault Inlet was no good and that the Company would do far better to site Australind at a spot *he'd* discovered, north of Perth.

Grey's motive was probably to draw attention to his discoveries but his information was wrong. The land he'd discovered (near present-day Geraldton) was far inferior to the green and well-watered country at Leschenault Inlet. Incredibly, the directors of the Western Australian Company took Grey on trust and, without waiting to check his claims, they issued a statement that Australind would now be founded at a new and wonderful site north of Perth.

Public confidence in the Company immediately collapsed, and no wonder. This amazing switch, after all the grand claims and the detailed plans already issued on the basis that the settlement would be at Leschenault Inlet, made it apparent that the Company didn't know about Australia and didn't know what they were doing.

Australind, it now seemed, had been no more than an idea which was waiting to happen somewhere, somehow. The investors determined that it would not happen at their expense and they pulled out in droves. The Western Australian Company had collected £65 000 from preliminary sales of land; it was now asked to return more than half that money. Whatever else it may have been, the Company was not a fraud and it paid back all the money, plus interest. But it now faced a desperate shortage of funds to develop the colony and, just to complicate things, at this moment its bankers collapsed.

Most of this happened while Marshall Waller Clifton was on the high seas with his first body of colonists. On arrival in Western Australia it only took him a day to establish that Grey's claims were ridiculous and he proceeded to establish the Australind colony at Leschenault Inlet.

But it was already doomed. The news that the Company was now back to the place they'd first thought of did nothing to restore confidence in London, while the colonists who'd actually gone to Australind were dismayed by what they found there. The Company's initial propaganda had been so effective thay they had in their minds' eye a solid, established settlement; but all they could see was a couple of surveyors' huts in a tract of virgin bush.

They were not the sort of colonists who expected to fell trees and clear bush. The plan was for labourers to do that. But the emigrant labourers they'd brought quickly cleared out for more civilised parts and there was no local labour. The gentry tried to tame the wilderness themselves but it was too much for them.

The chief victim of the collapse was Marshall Waller Clifton. In 1843, just three years after that memorable farewell speech to the surveyors in London, he was forced to gather them together again in the Survey

building at Australind and make another farewell speech. The Company had instructed him to disband the surveying establishment.

Waller Clifton himself stayed on at Australind; he was one of the very few original settlers to do so. His descendants still live there and the Clifton home, Upton House, is one of the few reminders in the seaside village of Australind of that original great enterprise. Other reminders are an old wooden inn, sadly decrepit now, an early settler's shack which is the Church of St Nicholas, Australind, the smallest church in Western Australia, and the graveyard where many Cliftons have been buried over the past century.

Marshall Waller Clifton suffered badly from the failure of the Australind scheme and inscribed on his headstone are the bitter words:

'Another race will succeed us and reap that golden harvest which we might have enjoyed.'

And down by the shore of Leschenault Inlet, which was to be the Port of Australind, is a plaque which tells quite succinctly how Marshall Waller Clifton's golden dream started, and how it ended.

One can look at Australind as a grand idea, wrecked by the mischievous George Grey, just as Macquarie's grand ideas were wrecked by another small man of Australian history, Mr Bigge. Or one can see Australind as a laughable idea, a folly perpetrated by confident, ignorant men who understood nothing about Australia.

But like so many of the other things that went wrong in Australian history, it wasn't laughable for those who lost their fortunes and broke their hearts. The plaque that tells of the death of the Australind dream ends with a sentence that is the best epitaph for all the dreams that shattered on the rocky shores of Australian practicality:

'THE ACHIEVEMENT FELL SHORT OF THE VISION.'

left: **In Memory of the Pioneers, Willowie, South Australia**

opposite: **Twofold Bay at night**

BEN BOYD

'If you can look into the seeds of time
And say which grain will grow and which
will not . . .'

MACBETH

Of all those in Australia who aspired to scale the heights of fame and fortune, there were few who aimed so high, or failed so narrowly, as Benjamin Boyd.

Boyd is one of the most compelling and most mysterious figures in Australian history. Many of his secrets died with him, but in the story that we know there are interesting parallels with the story of Macbeth: Boyd, too, was driven by vaulting ambition; there was a woman involved; and his adventure ended in disaster and violent death.

He was the second son of Edward Boyd of Merton Hall, Wigtonshire, Scotland, and he began a career as a stockbroker in London in the 1820s. Whether he became a wealthy man at this time is questionable, like so much of his career, but he certainly managed to convey an impression of wealth. He was influential and well connected and claimed to be on intimate terms with certain members of the Royal Family. He had a palatial yacht, the *Wanderer,* and he managed to gain membership of the Royal Yacht Club, which was a golden key to the world of wealth and privilege. He also had financial interests in the St George Steam Packet Company and it was evidently his interest in shipping and trade which first attracted him to the commercial possibilities of New South Wales.

A chance conversation in the London Balloonists Club (an appropriate setting, perhaps, for the birthplace of the gigantic balloons that he was later to float) alerted Boyd to potential profits to be made from a coastal shipping service between Port Jackson, Port Phillip and Van Diemen's Land. Whaling was one of Australia's most important primary industries in early days, and Boyd also heard mention of the whaling possibilities at a place called Twofold Bay.

In 1840 he wrote to Lord John Russell, stating that he was about to inaugurate a steamship service on the eastern coast of Australia, and requesting permission from the British Government to select half a dozen locations on the coast for harbours and coaling stations with the right to buy adjacent land. Boyd also informed the British Government of a grand plan that he had in mind to develop a Pacific Island colony, which could be expected to become a significant addition to the British Empire, with Boyd himself at its head.

Thus, before his Australian adventure began Boyd revealed a glimpse of the extraordinary ambition that spurred him. Although he was to be remembered as a soldier of fortune, he was no ordinary fortune-seeker — he sought to become a Prince. Why? One can surmise that his ambition was not unconnected with his failed romance with a Miss Emma Green, daughter of London shipping magnate, Sir William Green. Boyd proposed to her and, with all his suavity and charm, was rejected. It seems that her family, and perhaps Miss Emma herself, felt that the only suitable husband would be a man of rank and title. Boyd was well-born but he was not a member of the aristocracy. It may be that this slight to his pride determined him to gain by his own efforts the honours which had not been bestowed on him as a birthright. Ben Boyd was a man who was trying to prove something to himself, to the world, and perhaps not least to Miss Emma Green.

The British Government's answer to his proposals was less than Boyd had hoped. He was told that every favourable consideration would be given to his requests by Governor Gipps of New South Wales but that it was really a matter for the Governor. Boyd pressed on, no doubt determined to win from the Colonial Government the favours that the British Government refused to grant him. With a group of well-known London businessmen he floated the Royal Bank of Australia. Its announced capital was one million pounds and investors, lured by promises of handsome returns, eagerly subscribed for shares. At the same time, with his brother Mark, Ben Boyd set up a series of interlocking private companies which ensured that the Boyd brothers would get several bites at the revenue of the business which was to be nominally conducted between Australia and England by the Royal Bank.

He then despatched to Sydney three paddle-steamers, *Seahorse, Juno* and *Cornubia* all carrying supplies for his ventures. These ships were obtained from the St George Steam Packet Company which went into liquidation in 1843. Boyd represented himself in New South Wales as the owner of these ships but in the bankruptcy proceedings of Mark Boyd, after Ben's death, it emerged that the ships had not been paid for and large sums of money were owed to the defunct St George Steam Packet Company.

The colonials could not know this at the time and when Ben Boyd himself arrived in Sydney Harbour in the *Wanderer,* on July 18, 1842, it was to a rousing welcome. The Sydney citizens were agog at the news that a financial colossus was arriving amongst them and they crowded the heights of Sydney Harbour to view the entry of the *Wanderer.*

Boyd had left nothing to chance. Somewhere in life he had learned the importance of first impressions, and he made sure that the colonial press was well supplied with news of his great plans and his impending arrival. The *Juno, Seahorse* and *Cornubia* were waiting to greet him in Sydney Harbour and another of his ships, the *Velocity,* fired a pre-arranged gun salute.

The *Wanderer,* Boyd's ace card, overwhelmed the spectators. Described as a 'yacht', she was actually a very fast topsail schooner of eighty-four tons. She carried fifteen gleaming cannon, a picked crew of fourteen, and was most lavishly fitted out. Boyd had had the pleasure of entertaining Royalty to dinner on board her during gatherings of the Royal Yacht Squadron at Cowes. As a unit of the Royal Yacht Squadron, the *Wanderer* enjoyed all the privileges of a man-of-war, could enter or leave any British port without hindrance, and could anchor wherever she pleased. Boyd took immediate advantage of these privileges by dropping anchor in Farm Cove, the prime anchorage of Port Jackson.

As a final touch, all his ships flew his house flag, two honey-bees depicted in blue on a white ground. This flag, designed by Boyd himself, was a play on his initials B. B. and on his industrious habits. Ben was indeed a busy bee. Hollywood, a century later, would have called him a 'go-getter'. (And if Ben, with his flair for publicity, had been round a century later, there's no doubt he'd have taken Hollywood to the cleaners.)

The entry into Sydney Harbour was beautifully stage-managed and it had the desired effect. Ben Boyd was immediately spoken of as the most important man in Australia and there was little doubt in the public mind that he was also the richest. He was known to have brought some of the Royal Bank's million pound capital, perhaps all of it, with him to Australia on the *Wanderer.*

Boyd wasted no time in capitalising on this favourable impression. He quickly made contact with the most important people in the colony and, within a few weeks, he had set up the Sydney office of the Royal Bank at Church Hill and was advertising the operations of the bank in the Sydney press.

This was a misleading beginning as the Royal Bank was never to operate as a conventional bank in Australia. Instead, Boyd set out to build a mercantile and pastoral empire. He launched the *Seahorse* on a cargo run between Sydney, Melbourne and Launceston. He also started negotiating to acquire leases of stations and he moved so rapidly that, within three years, he was the biggest landholder in the country, apart from the Crown, with twenty stations in the Monaro, Riverina and Port Phillip districts.

Most of these holdings were in the name of the Royal Bank of Australia, but Boyd held some of the most important stations, as well as a number of his other important enterprises, in his own name. The actual amount of Royal Bank funds which he had brought to Australia was £200 000, though if the colonials thought it was a million pounds he was prepared to let them think so. The extent of his own private funds is unknown, but there is little doubt that some of the Royal Bank's funds were used to finance Boyd's private ventures.

At Neutral Bay, Sydney, Boyd had his stores and wharf and wool-washing establishment where his wool clips were prepared for shipping to London. He also lived there in a grand mansion called Craignathan. The mansion has gone now, but Ben Boyd Road in Neutral Bay is named for him.

The keystone of Boyd's enterprises, however, was not Sydney, but a harbour called Twofold Bay, halfway down the coast to Melbourne.

above: Southern Shores, Twofold Bay

below: Skeleton of Old Tom, Eden Museum

With Oswald Brierly, who had accompanied him from London on the *Wanderer* and who was later to become marine artist to Queen Victoria, Boyd landed in Twofold Bay in 1842 near the mouth of the Nullica River.

There was already a settlement on the northern side of Twofold Bay, a small whaling station and village called Eden, established by the pioneering Imlay brothers. But Boyd scorned the tiny struggletown of Eden; he had something grander in mind. South of Eden, a new Xanadu was to rise — no shanty-town but a real city, perhaps a future capital of Australia. It was to be called, naturally, Boydtown. In his diary, Brierly recorded that Boyd, standing on the dazzling white sand of the beach, made a grand speech and exhorted Brierly: 'Imagine ourselves the founders of a second Rome!' He went on to point out with elation the various places and features of the locality which would bear their names, and pass them down to future generations.

Building a second Rome was to prove a slower and costlier operation than Boyd had ever imagined, but he drew up plans, despatched scores of stonemasons and bricklayers and carpenters from Sydney, and within a year of his arrival in the colony the construction of Boydtown was under way. Although its distance from Sydney presented Boyd with unexpected difficulties and delays in obtaining labour and building materials, it was nevertheless an astute choice for his operations. It was a marvellous natural harbour; it was the logical port for the Monaro district, where Boyd was in the process of acquiring thousands of acres of rich grazing land; and the oceans around it abounded in whales.

There was much money to be made from whaling. In the earliest days of the colony, before the growth of the wool trade, whale products had been the major export commodity, and many foreign whalers had been attracted to Australian waters by the rich prospects. Twofold Bay had been in use for years before Boyd arrived, both as a shore whaling station and as a base for deep sea whalers to boil out the oil from whale carcasses at try-works.

Boyd included both these operations in his Twofold Bay enterprises. He made it the supply base for a fleet of whalers which ventured far out to sea, while at East Boyd, just inside the southern headland of the bay, he established a whaling station under the supervision of his friend, Oswald Brierly.

Boydtown itself, while it was certainly intended to be a monument to the high-flying Benjamin, was no mere architectural folly. It was meant to be a living, working town, and the centrepiece of Boyd's commercial scheme, welding together his triple ventures in grazing, shipping and whaling. The first substantial building completed at Boydtown was the Seahorse Inn, named for the ship that he had trading on the coastal run. An advertisement appearing in Sydney papers in 1843 announced:

> 'For the convenience of Passengers going to and returning from Maneroo, this Hotel will be completed in a few weeks, and will be conducted in a manner calculated to give satisfaction to the public, and as nearly as possible at English prices.'

Within the next few years, the inn was joined by other buildings calculated to establish Boyd's empire on solid ground — stores, wharves, woolsheds, boiling-down works, even a church.

By the middle of the 1840s Ben Boyd was close to achieving his aim of raising himself to the aristocracy. He was grazing one hundred and eighty thousand sheep and cattle on his pastoral empire, and, in colonial terms, he was already a kind of Emperor. He was known as the 'Prince of Squatters', and even enjoyed the privilege of issuing his own banknotes, in denominations from five shillings to one pound. They were headed:

'BOYD. TWOFOLD BAY OR SYDNEY'

Boyd had cut a most amazing dash in the colony in a short time, and he was for a short time much admired. A Sydney paper in 1843 published this encomium: 'There is no individual who has done so much for the Colony and in so short a time as Mr Benjamin Boyd. If we had more such men, the Colony would soon go ahead.'

To a considerable degree, Boyd deserved this tribute. He had certainly shown a shrewd eye for commercial possibilities that had escaped gentlemen of longer colonial experience, but less energetic disposition. He had injected funds and confidence into the colony at a time when it badly needed both. And, at Boydtown, he had launched a bold and costly gamble. It very nearly came off. Launched earlier, or later, it might well have succeeded, and made a fortune for its sponsor. But Ben Boyd, one of the classic gamblers of Australian history, had played his cards at the wrong time. A financial depression was already underway when he arrived in New South Wales and the depression deepened as the 1840s wore on. It was one of those depressions endemic to Australia, and to other countries, that relied on a limited number of exports to support their standard of living. For a complication of reasons, overseas prices for Australian exports fell. Inevitably, home prices began to fall too.

This should not have troubled Ben Boyd as he had been extremely fortunate in his early pastoral dealings. In Monaro it was said that he had bought his sheep for tenpence a head,

below: **Ruins of Ben Boyd's Church, Boydtown**

with the stations thrown in for nothing. The licence fees that he was paying for his vast runs amounted to one penny per thousand acres.

Boyd and his fellow pastoralists in the New South Wales Legislative Council (he was elected President of the Pastoralists' Association in 1844, and represented the Port Phillip District in the Legislative Council from 1844 to 1845) thought that even this wasn't good enough. Harking back to the good old days when rich tracts of Australia were given away for nothing, they thought that they should be granted freehold rights to their vast leases and be permitted to run their stock there forever, for nothing.

George Gipps, the Governor of New South Wales, had other ideas. He was not in sympathy with the squatting interests and he thought it was quite absurd and inequitable that one man, such as Ben Boyd, should be allowed to control dozens of huge runs for the payment of a single annual licence fee which

amounted to a trifle. Gipps proposed instead that the squatters should pay an annual licence fee of ten pounds for each station they held. He defined a station as an area of twenty square miles with not more than four thousand sheep or five hundred cattle. Moreover, the squatters, to enjoy a continuing right to their runs, would be required to buy a block of three hundred and twenty acres every eight years, at the price of one pound an acre.

The squatters were horrified. Boyd pointed out that he would have to pay the government £6 400 every eight years merely for the purchase of blocks on his twenty stations. The truth was that many of the pastoralists could not have afforded to buy the land they were squatting on, while those who could had no intention of doing so. They saw no reason to pay good money for what they had come to regard as their own and what they expected to keep for virtually nothing.

The cry was raised in the Legislative Council that a tax was being levied upon the people without its consent, and that the Government

below: **Ben Boyd's Tower, South Head, Twofold Bay**

was threatening to become 'the Executioner of its own subjects'. Gipps was prevented from introducing his new measures but the public controversy surrounding all this showed Ben Boyd and his fellow-squatters in a poor light.

The 'people' of New South Wales were not solely comprised of squatters, though many of the Legislative Councillors liked to think they were. The colony was now sixty years old and there was a substantial class of free labourers, both immigrant and native-born. To their mind, the squatting interest was grossly *under* taxed. What was more, the squatting interest was attempting to reduce their wages and conditions and one of the leading lights in this repressive movement was Benjamin Boyd. Boyd's pastoral labourers, it was said, worked for 'sixpence a week, a Kilmarnock cap and shirt, and indifferent rations'. As early as 1843, he had told a select committee on immigration that he employed upwards of two hundred shepherds and stockmen, but despaired of the colony's prosperity 'unless we have cheap labour, and can bring the wages of the shepherd who will undertake large flocks to £10 a year with rations.'

Since the prevailing pastoral wage was already double the figure that Boyd had nominated, and since his idea of rations included only meat and flour — tea and sugar he considered luxuries — his remarks were not popular in working class and liberal quarters. One of his colonial critics, Samuel Sydney, thought they were typical of 'the haughty gentlemanly, selfish class he represented'. Students of Ben Boyd's career and ambitions — and he was such a compelling figure that he quickly attracted such students — began to see that Boyd did not care for other people and was more than willing to make his fortune at other people's expense.

Boyd himself, naturally, saw it differently. It was certainly his intention to make life easy for himself, but he couldn't see why it should be easy for people less special than himself, and he reduced the conditions of his workers to the point that he was unable to inspect his own stations without a police escort.

This might have given a less single-minded man pause for consideration, but Ben Boyd developed an obsession with the idea of cheap labour. Certainly, the free labour forces in New South Wales were proving hard to attract to Boyd's outposts, but, at a time when resistance to the importation of convicts was reaching its peak in New South Wales, Boyd proposed that Boydtown, where he'd already enjoyed the benefits of some cheap convict labour, should become a new convict depot.

When the Government failed to respond to this appeal, Boyd despatched a whaling ship to the New Hebrides to recruit native labour. This act was represented as an overflow of the milk of human kindness — 'As a philanthropist, I cannot imagine a greater benefit conferred on a race than removing these poor benighted creatures from a state of starvation and heathen ignorance to a Christian country' — but it was not seen as such by the fiery Robert Lowe, who rose in the Legislative Council and denounced what he called 'the commencement of a slave-trade in the Pacific'.

Boyd's importation of Pacific Islanders from Tanna and Lifu must have seemed to him a good idea at the time, but it turned out to be his most disastrous experiment in public relations. The Islanders, who had been beguiled by unknown promises to Australian shores, did not like what they found at Boyd's stations and they ran away in droves.

They arrived in large numbers in the streets of Sydney, scandalising the good citizens by their jabbering and their unholy state of nakedness. According to reports of the time, when questioned about their grievances they pointed to their stomachs and growled 'Missa Boyd'. Perhaps they were complaining about the meagre tucker allowance on Ben Boyd's stations; perhaps they were forecasting a Pacific Island revenge on the gentleman. In any case, they were repatriated to their islands.

Boyd might have survived the accusation that he was a slave-trader — the importation of Pacific Islanders was revived in Queensland in the 1860s and prospered mightily for forty years — but by 1847 he was in even more serious trouble. Despite his undoubted talents as a promoter and financial manipulator, Boyd was not an expert in the management of stations or stock and his bloated pastoral empire got out of hand. He was also unlucky in his shipping ventures and suffered a costly insurance loss when the *Seahorse* was wrecked in the Tamar River, while at Boydtown his pet project for a township was draining away revenue because of the extravagance and financial manipulations of the managers he'd appointed.

The upshot was that Boyd misrepresented to London the prices that he had obtained for sheep and cattle at Australian sales. The discrepancy was picked up when one of the London directors of the Royal Bank noted that the prices quoted in the Sydney press were much lower than those that Boyd had reported.

The Royal Bank began to suspect that they were in trouble. And indeed they were. William Sprott Boyd, Benjamin's brother, was sent out from London to depose him as Australian director of the Royal Bank. Sprott Boyd found that the Royal Bank was not only rapidly losing money but that its affairs were inextricably tangled with those of Ben Boyd. Sprott Boyd was unable to unravel the situation and he in turn was replaced by a liquidator in 1849. The Royal Bank of Australia was finished. The shareholders eventually discovered that not only had they lost all their original capital, but they were required to put up a further substantial sum of money to pay off the Bank's debts.

Ben Boyd's movements, after his downfall from the Royal Bank, are obscure. He was allowed to keep some of the enterprises that were in his own name and he dickered with some new schemes, including one for a gold-mine in the Carcoar region of New South Wales.

If anybody understood the entanglement of the Boyd affairs and knew which things rightfully belonged to the Royal Bank and which to Benjamin, that person can only have been Benjamin himself. And by 1849 Benjamin must have known which way the wind was blowing. He had suffered the humiliation of being summonsed to Darlinghurst Gaol on a charge that he had not paid wages due to his Boydtown overseer, Moutry. It must have been a ghastly comedown for a man who, just a few years earlier, had entertained the cream of colonial society and been described as the most eligible bachelor in New South Wales.

It is reputed that the first discovery of gold in New South Wales was by an Anglican clergyman, W. E. Clarke, near Hartley in 1841, that he showed his specimens of gold to Sir George Gipps and that the Governor told him, 'Put it away, Mr Clarke, or we shall all have our throats cut!'.

Certainly, Ben Boyd had received no news of gold in New South Wales by 1849. The Belubula Goldmine, in which he had an interest, turned out a dud. But then came the news of the gold strike in California, on the Sacramento River near the fishing village of San Francisco. Boyd quietly slipped out of Sydney Harbour on the *Wanderer,* bound for California. On the way out, he lost his bow anchor — 'a parting legacy', he wrote, 'to the colony in which I had hoped for so much, and though in part succeeded, yet in the main failed through little of my own fault.'

He was never to return to Australia. It appears that, before leaving, he had sold off everything that was his, or that he could represent as his, for ready cash. He must have taken to California more gold than he found there because, by every account, his venture to the American goldfields was a failure.

Yet he was able to maintain his expensive establishment on the *Wanderer* for a year and a half and in June, 1851, to refit it for his last and maddest adventure. According to his captain on the *Wanderer,* John Webster, Boyd sailed away from San Francisco determined to found some principality in the Pacific Islands. In Australia, he had been first called the 'Prince of Squatters'. When he imported coloured labour, he was reviled as the 'Prince of Darkness'. Now, he dreamed of becoming 'Prince of the Papuan Confederation'.

On October 15, 1851, Boyd went ashore at Guadalcanal in the Solomon Islands to shoot game. A couple of shots were heard and Boyd was never seen again. His fate was not princely; it is more likely that he became the main course at a cannibal feast as foreseen by those Pacific Islanders in Sydney who had rubbed their bellies and growled 'Missa Boyd!'.

The *Wanderer* extricated itself from Guadalcanal after a pitched battle with natives in war canoes. She limped back to Australia one month later, but was wrecked in a storm off Port Macquarie. The portrait of Emma

Green was amongst the wreckage recovered from the yacht. Ever since he'd left England, Ben Boyd, that eligible bachelor at whom all the colonial belles of Sydney set their caps, had kept this portrait concealed in a secret compartment of his cabin on the *Wanderer*.

In seven years, Ben Boyd swept through the colony of New South Wales like a storm, and his traces were soon hard to find. Of all his enterprises, only whaling had proved consistently profitable to him, and it was the only one to survive him. Whaling was carried on at Twofold Bay for nearly a century, chiefly by the Davidson family, whose ancestor came to Boydtown to work for Ben Boyd. Now the whaling industry is finished there and all that is left to show for it is a ruined try-works, the skeleton of Tom, the killer whale, and some artefacts in the Eden Museum.

And of all the monuments that Ben Boyd hoped would survive in his 'second Rome', and carry his name down to future generations, just three survive. One is his Tower, on the South Head of Twofold Bay. Built at vast expense from Pyrmont sandstone hauled all the way from Sydney by bullock wagon, it never functioned as the lighthouse that Boyd intended because, with typical arrogance, he insisted that it would be lit only for his own ships and the Government would not agree to let it operate under those rules.

Another is his church, built high on a ridge to dominate his dream city. Although it was the scene of one christening and two burials, the church was never furnished and never consecrated, and it looms on the hillside now as a roofless ruin.

The third surviving relic of Ben Boyd, and the only one that modern tourists will find still in use, is the Seahorse Inn. Described in Ben's time as 'a splendid hotel in the Elizabethan style', it has endured some extraordinary ups and downs since 1842. It has, at various times, been stripped and vandalised and practically ruined. More recently, it has been the subject of grand renovation projects, announced but unrealised.

I hope that somebody will eventually restore the Seahorse Inn as an historic inn, in Ben Boyd's style. Whether or not you approve of Ben Boyd, you can't but wonder at this meteoric figure of Australia's past. And, if the new Seahorse Inn should contain a Swashbucklers' Tavern, or a Buccaneers' Bar, then I expect the ghost of Benjamin Boyd will be a frequent guest.

below: **The Seahorse Inn, Boydtown**

opposite: **The Darling River**

THE DARLING RIVER

Sir Ralph Darling, who arrived to govern New South Wales in December, 1825, intended at first to remain impartial between the two conflicting colonial factions, the exclusives and the emancipists.

He had been especially warned to be careful of that most dangerous of men, John Macarthur, the leader of the exclusives. By a curious coincidence, Macarthur called on Darling soon after his arrival and informed the Governor that he (Macarthur) had determined to destroy Mr Howe, the editor of the *Sydney Gazette,* because he didn't like the way that newspaper had mentioned him. Macarthur added meaningly that he had 'never yet failed in ruining a man who had become obnoxious to him'. Darling was left in no doubt that this general threat encompassed Governors as well as ordinary men. The curious coincidence in all this was that Darling was to ruin his career in New South Wales by taking the same course of action that Macarthur had blustered about — by attacking the press.

Darling was a stiff professional soldier whose natural sympathies were with the Tories and against the radical factions who, with W. C. Wentworth at their head, were fighting for representative government, trial by jury and guaranteed freedom of the press. Darling frankly did not understand this agitation. As he saw it, New South Wales was a convict colony. The rights that free men might enjoy in a free society could not apply here, and it was unrealistic to ask for them.

But it was one particular event that ended Darling's attempt at impartiality, precipitated him into the arms of the exclusives and caused the other side to heap scorn on his head. In November, 1826, two soldiers called Sudds and Thompson made the decision that a convict's lot was better than a soldier's lot, and they committed robbery in the hope of being caught.

They were caught, and their sentence was seven years on the road gang. They were drummed out of their regiment and thrown into irons, including an iron collar with spikes projecting from it. Sudds, unfortunately, was in a bad state of health, suffering from tumors, and after a few days in the monstrous iron collar, he died. There was an outcry from the popular press, namely Wentworth's and

Wardell's *Australian* and Edward Smith Hall's *Monitor.* Wentworth addressed a public meeting in Sydney where his remarks about the example of America in 1776, and the necessity for New South Wales to shake off the yoke of tyranny, were greeted with roars of approval.

Darling, angered by the criticism and frightened by the overtones of seditious republicanism, replied by trying to muzzle the press. He introduced Acts requiring newspapers to be licensed by the government. The licences would be forfeited if the proprietor or publisher were found guilty of a blasphemous or seditious libel. The exclusives, who hated the popular press, were delighted with these proposed laws. But to their fury, and to Darling's, Chief Justice Forbes refused to grant the required certificate for the legislation. He said it was repugnant to English law.

The *Monitor* and the *Australian* hailed Forbes as the champion of freedom and proceeded to make things as hot as they could for Governor Darling. Smith Hall employed the columns of the *Monitor* to accuse Darling of tyranny 'surpassed only by that of the Great Mogul, the Czar of Muscovy and the Emperor of China'. Darling returned the compliment by making things as hot as possible for the press and Smith Hall spent time behind bars for seditious libel. But public feeling was increasingly against Darling.

At a dinner of the Turf Club in Sydney, when the toast was proposed to the exports of the colony, a voice was clearly heard to say, 'And may General Darling be the first of them'. This was a specially barbed insult because Governor Darling attended the Turf Club as its Honorary President.

When, to his own great chagrin, Governor Darling was recalled in 1831, there was general jubilation in Sydney. Wentworth and his supporters roasted an ox and six sheep at a celebration at Vaucluse, while a band played the mocking air 'Over the Hills and Far Away'. And on the day that Darling boarded the *Hooghly* to depart from Sydney Harbour, the *Monitor* came out with an announcement, in huge capitals:

'HE'S OFF!
THE REIGN OF TERROR ENDED.'

But the Governor had left his mark on the

colony. His name had been given to Australia's longest river as well as to such other features of Australia as Darling Harbour and the Darling Downs. It is one of the ironies of Australian History that people in later times often imagined that the Darling River had earned its name as a term of endearment towards the river itself. It was, in fact, named for a Governor who had signally failed to endear himself to his subjects.

Once the Blue Mountains had been crossed the next great mystery in Australian exploration centred on the rivers that flowed westward from the Great Dividing Range. Did they dwindle away in remote deserts, did they pour into an inland sea or did they perhaps flow into a more distant and greater river? In 1817 and 1818 Governor Macquarie sent out his Surveyor-General, John Oxley, to follow the course of the rivers that had been named for the Governor, the Lachlan and the Macquarie. On both occasions Oxley was foiled. The rivers appeared to lose themselves in a morass of swamps and marshes.

The year 1828 was a year of drought and Governor Darling reasoned that it might now be possible to bypass the swamps and discover the secret of the western rivers. He sent his military secretary, Captain Charles Sturt, on this expedition accompanied by the native-born explorer, Hamilton Hume, and a party of eleven other men.

Sturt's party followed the course of the Macquarie from Wellington to the marshes where, once again, the river channel disappeared in a maze of reeds. Casting further west Sturt reached another stream on January 1, 1829, and named it New Year's Creek. (Mitchell subsequently renamed it the Bogan River.) Following this stream, he came next day to a large river which he was convinced was the river into which the north-western streams flowed. He named it the Darling after the benefactor who had sent him on this expedition. To the great surprise and disappointment of Sturt's thirsty men, when they cupped their hands and tried to drink the river water they found it was salt. The cause was salt springs in the river but another idea suggested itself to Sturt, an idea that was to become something of a tragic obsession with him — the notion of an inland sea.

The explorers followed the Darling about seventy miles downstream but beyond establishing that it flowed towards the south-west they were no wiser as to its ultimate destination. They did, however, satisfy themselves before returning to Sydney that the Castlereagh River also flowed into the Darling.

In the next year, Darling sent Sturt back into the bush to follow the course of the Murrumbidgee River and Sturt proceeded to solve the mystery of the western rivers in one of the epic feats of Australian exploration. He established that all the rivers flowed eventually into the Murray River, and that the Murray River flowed into the sea at Encounter Bay on the southern coast of Australia.

There was just one slight question-mark over Sturt's findings. After his whaleboat was shot like a cork from the Murrumbidgee into the broad Murray, Sturt had proceeded down the river and at one point had seen a new and beautiful river coming into the Murray from the north. After a short journey up this river, Sturt was confident that it was the same stream which he had encountered in its upper reaches a year earlier and named the Darling.

But he had not *proved* that it was the same river, and in Sydney there sat a man whose heart burned with envy of Sturt, and whose chief desire, apart from achieving personal glory, was to prove Sturt wrong. He was Major Thomas Livingstone Mitchell, who had become Surveyor-General in 1828 and who had pestered Governor Darling to be allowed to go out and discover something. To his fury, Darling had told him to stay home and mind the office and had sent Sturt out instead.

Mitchell had been a cartographer in the Peninsular War and, through his competence in surveying and map-making, he was to make valuable contributions eventually to the general body of knowledge about Australia. But he was as unpleasant a man as Sturt was a pleasant one; utterly vain and self-centred, and given to the ignoble habit of denigrating other explorers and renaming features which they had already named. In later years a member of one of Mitchell's expeditions remarked that anyone anxious for a vision of Hell should try travelling through the wilds of Australia with the Major in charge.

above: **Sturt's Desert Pea**

below: **At Menindee Lakes**

Mitchell drove a succession of Governors mad with his requests to go out exploring, and, to gain peace, Darling's replacement, Governor Bourke, let him go. In 1831 Mitchell had already been out to investigate the Namoi and Gwydir Rivers, hoping to prove the theory of a man called Clarke the Barber. Clarke the Barber was a runaway convict who had lived with the Aborigines and who claimed they had told him that these rivers flowed into a giant river which crossed the entire continent and flooded into the sea on the north-west coast of Australia. Mitchell was greatly interested in this theory since, if true, it would make nonsense of the theories of his arch-rival, Sturt. But on investigation Mitchell was forced to conclude that Clarke the Barber was lying his head off.

In 1835 he decided to try a different tack and persuaded Governor Bourke to let him take an expedition to the Darling to check Sturt's discoveries. The expedition was armed to the teeth and Mitchell, as was his habit, rode at the head of it in full dress uniform and with military sword. His first act upon arriving

at the Darling was to erect a log stockade for protection against the hostile Aborigines. There is no evidence that they *were* hostile at this point, but Mitchell's behaviour was guaranteed to make them hostile soon enough. After hanging around for a fortnight at Fort Bourke, the stockade which he'd named for the Governor, Mitchell started off on his march downriver, a march designed to prove that Sturt was wrong and that the Darling did not flow into the Murray.

After 300 miles in which the Darling steadily flowed south-west towards the known position of the Murray, Mitchell was forced to conclude that the pestilential Sturt had been right after all. It looked as if the Darling *did* flow into the Murray. But Mitchell did not go on to the Murray to prove it. He abandoned his trek near the site of present-day Menindee, though not before a nasty affray in which his men shot up the Aborigines, and he returned to Sydney in a rage.

Nothing now remains of Major Mitchell's stockade at Fort Bourke except a plaque to show where it stood. But by the 1850s

pastoralists were moving along both banks of the upper Darling and a settlement formed at the end of the decade a few miles upstream from the stockade was called Bourke.

By this time the shape of the western river system was well established. It was known that the headwater of the Darling was the Severn River, which rose near Stanthorpe in Queensland, and became successively the Dumaresq, Macintyre, Barwon and finally the Darling. Numerous other rivers flowed into the headwaters, but the Darling proper was considered to begin with the junction of the Barwon and Culgoa Rivers in New South Wales. With its tributaries it drained the vast area of a quarter of a million square miles in two States.

The first settlement on the river below the Barwon-Culgoa junction was Bourke and it thus gained the reputation of being the highest town on the Darling. It soon gained other kinds of reputation. The first riverboat arrived in 1859 and the first building arrived about the

below: **Sturt's first sight of the Darling River**

same time. It was, naturally, a pub. Less likely, it was run by an American. Sly's, or Tattersalls as it was later called, was a low-roofed, split-timber shanty in the roughest of bush traditions, but once it adorned the banks of the Darling it acted as a magnet, and other buildings were soon scattered around it. They were rough-and-ready structures, inhabited by a pretty rough-and-ready people. Bourke was a long way from the centres of civilised settlement, but as the surrounding country filled up with pastoralists it became the market and transport centre for a huge grazing area.

Bourke's strategic position was enhanced when the first bridge across the Darling was built there in 1883. Across that bridge the Cobb and Co. coaches ran up to Hungerford in Queensland; horse and bullock and mule trains, and camel teams driven by turbaned Afghans, hauled in the woolclip from the remote stations beyond the Warrego and the Paroo.

Under the bridge, which had a lifting centre span, river steamers passed to and fro with their cargoes, some from as far upriver as the Queensland border. At Bourke, they loaded and unloaded at a great wharf, three decks high, where three cranes were kept perpetually busy. Riverboats operated to Bourke from 1859 right up to the last visit of the *J. G. Arnold* in 1931. Many of these paddle-steamers had romantic names, such as *The Wandering Jew,* and some carried mysterious cargoes. A gentleman in clerical attire, who travelled down from Bourke in a steamer and impressed all on board by his piety, was later discovered to have been the bushranger, Frank Gardiner.

But the most famous, or notorious, voyage to Bourke was the cruise of the *Jane Eliza.* She set off from Morgan in May, 1883, with building materials that had been ordered for a new hotel in Bourke. *Jane Eliza* ran into one of the Darling's most drastic low rivers and was stranded in a succession of waterholes. It was stuck so long in one waterhole that the captain harnessed his power to running a riverside sawmill and cutting timber for a living.

When the river finally rose enough to let the *Jane Eliza* steam to Bourke it was June, 1886 — three years and one month after he'd started — and the world had changed. The railway had arrived at Bourke nine months before, building materials had arrived from Sydney on the railway and the new hotel was already built. To make things worse, the man who'd ordered the original supplies from the *Jane Eliza* had left town. The captain could do nothing but auction off his hotel building materials and they were bought by a contractor who hauled them off by camel to Broken Hill, where they suffered the peculiarly incongruous fate of being used to build a church.

Meanwhile the *Jane Eliza* had a dramatic change of fortune. Having loaded up again at Bourke, she caught the peak of a Darling flood and with three barges of Darling wool and Broken Hill ore pushing her along, she thundered back to Morgan in three weeks. So the *Jane Eliza* established two river records — slowest trip up to Bourke and quickest trip back. It was a favourite story with rivermen for years afterwards, guaranteed to set them choking with laughter, slapping their thighs and drumming their heels on the deck.

Still, fluctuations in the river like that hardly helped the river trade. People wanted some degree of regularity and reliability, both in receiving their supplies and in getting their woolclips away. And the Darling was such an unlikely river that it seemed to be more often in an extreme state, whether through drought or flood, than in a state of normality.

The riverboats were good enough while there was no other link to markets and seaports except the slower and more expensive bullock teams. But once the railway arrived at Bourke in 1885 the riverboat days on the upper Darling were numbered. The railhead had been extended to Bourke expressly to cut off the downriver wool trade to Adelaide and to divert the western wool to Sydney. It did just that, and from the fleet of fifty steamers and barges that plied the Darling at the peak of the steamer trade, there was not one left operating by the 1930s.

The town of Bourke, however, prospered mightily from the coming of the railway. In the centre of an area that ran a million sheep, it became the biggest wool-despatching railhead in Australia. (It still is — 44 000 bales were sent away from Bourke Railway Station in 1976.) By the 1890s, Bourke was a booming stock town, freely spoken of as 'the Chicago of the

West'. It had two hundred businesses, three solicitors, five doctors, and twenty-two hotels where bush drifters like Henry Lawson could wash the dust from their throats. It was still, in many ways, a rugged frontier town. The streets were dirt, there were a thousand working bullocks in the town and, when the teamsters were passing through, Bourke was described as one giant stock-yard hidden under a blanket of dust. Its heat was notorious:

'The only message from the dead
That ever came distinctly through
Was "Send my overcoat to Hell"
It came to Bourke in '92.'

And it was famous as 'the end of the line', the last outpost on the western railway that stretched nearly 600 miles from Sydney. An otherwise undistinguished shearers' song called 'Gooriannawa' gained a reputation for having so many verses that it took the entire train trip from Sydney to Bourke to sing them all.

Henry Lawson and his mates would hardly recognise now the blazing dusty boomtown they knew in '92. Modern Bourke is a green, pleasant, quiet country town of 3 500 people. It hasn't had to face a severe water shortage since a weir was built on the Darling in 1897. And it is no longer the end of the line for railway passengers. Passenger trains ceased to operate to Bourke in 1975; the travel links now are by air or road.

Bourke was never the end of the road. It was always the focal point for roads running in from the far west, and even today it advertises itself as 'The Gateway to the Real Outback'. Out there, they will tell you, back of Bourke, beyond the Darling, lies the country where the crows fly backwards, the snakes bowl along like hoops and other less probable things happen.

But you don't have to go west of Bourke in search of improbabilities. There are plenty to be found south of Bourke, along the Darling River itself. Seventy miles downriver by road and about three times as far by the looping river lies the curiously named village of Louth, at about the spot where Captain Sturt turned back after exploring the Upper Darling. Jokers have suggested that Louth was named by a man with a lisp. But it was apparently named by a settler for his birthplace in Ireland.

On most days of the year, Louth is a sleepy little place, with a Post Office, a pub called Shindy's Inn, a few houses, and a population of about thirty-six, including cats and dogs. But on one day of the year, Louth springs to life as if electrified, and the population is increased one hundred times over. That is the Saturday in August when the Louth Turf Club holds its race meeting. On that day, people arrive from far and wide, some flying private planes from as far away as Victoria and South Australia.

Usually it's a five-race meeting with prize-money of about $4 000 and a plethora of bookies who also bet, of course, on the Sydney and Melbourne races. But there has to be more than that to attract three or four thousand people to this remote course every year. It's certainly not the track; the Louth Turf Club is the first to admit that the word 'Turf' is used loosely in Louth, and sometimes it's hard to see the horses for dust.

What distinguishes the Louth Picnic Races from hundreds of others in Australia is a special blend of hospitality, informality, foolery and fun that brings back the patrons year after year. The tables groan with goodies from the country kitchens of the Darling; the beer goes down like water never would; and the punters besiege the bookies, begging to be relieved of their bundles. After the races, there is a Grand Dance at Louth Hall, and after that, the revelry goes on as long as anyone can stay upright. It's quite an event, and it's the people of the Darling who make it.

At Dunlop Station, downriver from Louth, a vast shearing-shed still stands as a memorial to those huge Darling stations that made Australia, and themselves, rich in the nineteenth century. There were three million sheep along the river then. Dunlop, which was not the biggest station, covered nearly a million acres and at shearing time employed a hundred shearers and twelve cooks. Barney Murray, the present owner of Dunlop, says that in those days the sheep coming into the shed would stretch back in a string seventeen or eighteen miles long. In the early '80s, he says, they shore 360 000 sheep at Dunlop, and this incredible tally was achieved with hand shears, before Dunlop became the first Australian shed to introduce machine-shearing in 1886. In those years, Dunlop Station would send 10 000 bales of scoured wool overseas annually, and they sent them away by steamer. A steamer passed the wharf practically every day on its way upstream or down. Now the old Dunlop wharf is slowly slipping down the bank into the river.

Down at Wilcannia, the original town wharf is not much better preserved. You can stand on it, but at your own risk. And yet, this was a town that was once called 'the Queen of the Darling' and was reckoned to be the third most important port in the whole Murray-Darling River system. Wilcannia, unlike Bourke, was never joined to a railway system and for a long time practically everything went in and out of the town by riverboat.

On the Murray the riverboats have made a comeback in the past few years but on the Darling their traces have practically disappeared. I find this very sad; in fact, I find a town like Wilcannia very sad. The ghosts of an impressive past can be seen in its Post Office, its old Customs House and its Courthouse — solid and well-proportioned buildings that earned Wilcannia a reputation as a progressive town a century ago.

It was also famous far and wide for its large and formidable gaol where wild western characters dried out after sampling too generously the products of the German brewer, Resch. The Resch beer empire began in Wilcannia with a modest brewery which is now incorporated into the local Golf Club building.

below: **President of Louth Turf Club, Fon Duncan and Mrs Duncan**

Wilcannia was also the headquarters of the famous Darling emporium, Knox and Downs. In the days when Wilcannia was known as the capital of the Far West of New South Wales, Knox and Downs rode high and every grazier in the middle Darling had his account there. That was before a mining city called Broken Hill arose to steal Wilcannia's glory away.

The Knox and Downs store can still be inspected in Wilcannia. It was always known vulgarly as 'Ups and Downs' — a store that depends for its business on graziers is bound to witness, and suffer, changes of fortune. But Knox and Downs has evidently endured more downs than ups in recent years. It has a listless, decrepit feeling, like the town of Wilcannia itself. Perhaps Wilcannia will rise again some day to great things, but there is a still sad air that plays about the town; a murmur of lament for days and chances gone.

The last important settlement on the Darling River before Wentworth, where it joins the Murray, is the historic little town of Menindee. It was at this point that Major Mitchell turned away from the Darling in 1835 after one last nasty battle with its native tribes. It was through here, when it was called Laidley's Ponds, that Mitchell's great rival, Charles Sturt, passed in 1844 on his last attempt to find that great Inland Sea, and through here that he was carried back from that expedition in 1845, defeated and nearly dead of scurvy.

below: **Maiden's Hotel, Menindee**

And it was through Menindee, by this time established as a tiny settlement with one pub and one store, that Burke and Wills passed in 1860 on their way to that final disaster at Cooper's Creek. Some of their supplies were brought up to Menindee by riverboat, and they made it their base camp.

Burke and Wills slept in Room 10 of Payne's Menindee Hotel and their explorers' symbol, an arrow pointing north to the Gulf, can still be seen where they carved it on the verandah post near their room. It was perhaps the last night's good sleep that the unfortunate pair ever enjoyed. A. W. Howitt, passing through Menindee in 1861 in search of Burke and Wills, reported that Tom Payne's Hotel was a kind of explorers' club where the conversation centred on who was out and what country had been taken up. The bushmen, with beards, pipes and cabbage-tree hats, knowingly discussed the conduct and qualifications of explorers and inspected and criticised their stores and equipment.

The hotel, now a century and a quarter old, is no longer Payne's, but Maiden's Menindee Hotel. However that is an historic enough name in Menindee. The ancestors of the present proprietor, Jim Maiden, arrived in the town one year before Burke and Wills, and witnessed a few interesting scenes after Burke and Wills. The Yankee riverboat captain, Gus Pierce, recalled that, on one occasion when he arrived at Menindee, everyone in the pub was drinking ginger wine mixed with Worcester Sauce because nothing else was left to drink. Naturally he had no trouble unloading his entire cargo of English ale.

Menindee had gained quite a name by then. Locals tell a story of a travelling parson in those times who came upon an outback fencer, questioned him closely on his spiritual state, and eventually demanded: 'Look here, my man, have you ever been to Holy Communion?' The puzzled fencer scratched his head, thought a while and said, 'Holy Communion? Can't say I have.' Then he added quickly, 'But I've been to Menindee!' Perhaps that fencer came from Kinchega Station, just west of Menindee. It was one of the great old Darling stations, originally running from the river all the way west to the New South Wales border, and in over a

century of operation it shore some six million sheep. But the lease expired in 1967 and the station became Kinchega National Park, the fourth largest National Park in New South Wales. Now the wildlife and the vegetation have regenerated after their hundred-year war with sheep and rabbits and the land is back to the state that Sturt might have observed when he passed through it in 1844.

Before starting on that last expedition from Adelaide, Sturt had written: 'I have a strange idea that there may be a central sea not far from the Darling'. He was so confident of finding it that his seventeen-man party dragged along with them a whaleboat to sail the Central Sea and a Union Jack to plant on its shores.

What Sturt found instead, as he advanced into the unknown, was drought and desolation and eventual death for his lieutenant, Poole. He found the Stony Desert and the Simpson Desert and he was beaten back by some of the harshest country in the world. By the time he was carried back through Menindee in a state of paralysis, Adelaide had already given him up for dead. His whaleboat was abandoned in a creek bed, up near Milparinka.

From Menindee, Sturt had written: 'Tomorrow we start for the ranges, and then for the waters, the strange waters on which boat never swam and over which flag never floated.' It is curious to think how short a journey Sturt would have to make from Menindee now to find a sea where his whaleboat, and a thousand more, could sail. Within the Kinchega National Park, just a few miles from Menindee, there is now a sea, a man-made sea. It is the Menindee Lakes system and it contains a body of water three times bigger than Sydney Harbour. Unfortunately, it arrived too late for the gallant Captain Sturt. But it is, as he surmised it would be, not far from the river. It is fed by that implausible river which he christened, the Darling.

opposite: **Dead Man's Sandhill, Birdsville Track**

THE BIRDSVILLE TRACK

Where is 'the Real Outback'? It's a hard question to answer. In the Australian definitions of that territory, it is never where we are, but always somewhere else — it is 'back of beyond' or 'the country further out' or 'the Never Never'.

In his poem, *Ulysses*, Tennyson has his much-travelled Greek hero say:

'All experience is an arch where thro'
Gleams that untravelled world, whose margin fades
For ever and for ever when I move.'

The 'outback' seems to be like that. We march towards it as we would towards the future, but we can never reach it. When we reach the place we thought we were aiming for, it has become the present, the here and now. The future and the back of beyond, are still as far away as ever. And yet common sense tells us that 'the Real Outback' must lie on land, not at sea. Therefore if we cross and recross the continent of Australia from the northern seas to the Southern Ocean, from the Indian to the Pacific Ocean, we must encounter 'the Real Outback' somewhere.

I haven't traversed every inch of the Australian continent but I've seen enough of it to nominate my choice of location for 'the Real Outback'. And it is not in the centre of some vast desert, like the Gibson or the Great Victoria or the Great Sandy Desert, where even the nomadic Aborigines, with all their hunting skills, can barely survive. 'Outback' is not an Aboriginal word; it is not even a concept that makes any particular sense to Aborigines. 'Good land' and 'bad land' certainly came within their experience as they trekked about the continent, but 'outback'? Outback of what?

It is a white man's word, invented by colonial people who huddled together for safety in coastal cities and regarded the interior as hostile country. The further 'out' the country (actually they meant the further in from the coast), the more hostile they assumed it must be and the more remarkable and weird must be those white squatters who chose to live there. I take 'the Real Outback' to mean the most marginal area of pastoral settlement in Australia — a place where white men can make a living from the land, but the toughest possible place that they could find to do it. As it happens, that place is not Central Mount Stuart, a mountain north of Alice Springs which is the geographic centre of the Australian continent and therefore, by definition, the area most remote from the Australian coast. It is, instead, a tract of land running from the north of South Australia up to the border of that State with Queensland. It lies east of Lake Eyre, south-east of the Simpson Desert, and west of Sturt's Stony Desert. This is the country traversed by the legendary Birdsville Track and it has been classed as the most arid region to support permanent human settlement, not just in Australia, but in the world.

Here, for my money, is 'the Real Outback'. When Bourke, on the Darling River, advertises itself as the 'Gateway to the Real Outback', it is not to the Darling's western tributaries, the Warrego and the Paroo, that the indicators should be taken to point, but to a land much further west where a quite different river system drains into Lake Eyre through Cooper's Creek. The Cooper is formed by the combination of the Thomson River and the Barcoo River — a circumstance which has led to a typical outback joke. Out there, they say, everything is so big that it takes two rivers to make one creek.

It was in this country that Captain Sturt found himself in 1845, and it was no joking matter for him. His party, which passed within a few miles of the present site of Birdsville, encountered no inland sea but instead the Stony Desert, the Simpson Desert, and what Sturt called 'a landscape that never changed, except for the worse'. He found it difficult to believe that a benevolent God should have created such an appalling wilderness on the face of the earth.

It is no reflection on Sturt, but a generation was rising in Australia which knew more about bush survival than did British army officers with their cumbersome expeditionary parties and supply carts. Twenty-five years after Sturt's defeat and ten years after the abject deaths of Burke and Wills at Cooper's Creek, a small party of men rode into the same country from the north and emerged on the southern side with not only their skins intact, but with a mob of a thousand cattle which they had driven down all the way from Queensland.

The leader of this party was a stockman named Harry Redford and the cattle were stolen. Redford, a native of the Hawkesbury, had gone to Queensland to work in the cattle industry and in May, 1870, he lifted a thousand head of mixed cattle from Bowen Downs Station in Central Queensland. He had four associates but two of them left him soon afterwards. Redford and the other two men, in one of the most spectacular feats in the annals of Australian droving, brought the mob down the Thomson and Barcoo Rivers, and the Cooper and Strzelecki Creeks, through 1 500 miles of largely unknown country and eventually sold them in South Australia for five thousand guineas.

Redford made the mistake of picking up in his herd a pure white English stud bull. When a couple of equally skilled stockmen from Bowen Downs followed his trail down to South Australia — it had been a wet season and the track made by the mob was still visible — they were able to identify the white bull as one of a bunch purchased from Redford by a South Australian cattle station. Redford was arrested and taken to Roma in Queensland for trial. The evidence was pretty clear but Queensland juries were hard to convince in cases like these. Cattle-duffing was a pretty popular pastime when the victims were big stations. Besides, they may have felt that Redford had pulled off such a deed of daring that he deserved to get away with it.

Harry Redford was acquitted and carried shoulder-high from the court by his fans. The presiding judge, Judge Blakeney, thereupon made his famous remark to the jury: 'I thank God, gentlemen, that the verdict is yours, not mine.' He then suspended district court sessions at Roma for a period of two years. The episode captured the imagination of Rolf Boldrewood, whose novel *Robbery Under Arms* (1888) with its romantic hero, Captain Starlight, was based on Redford's exploits. Redford himself became a noted cattleman and overlanded the first stock from Queensland to Brunette Downs Station in the Northern Territory in 1883. He was drowned in a flooded Northern Territory Creek in 1901.

Redford was known as 'King of the Cattle-Duffers' and he was in no way ashamed of the title. He revealed in later years that he had been exceptionally lucky with the 1870 season. The sand dunes and stony plains had been covered with grass, the lake beds were full of clover, and the creeks were running. He had been able to navigate his way to the south by the sun and the flow of the waters. His one bad moment had been in the Cooper sandhills when he had sighted a dark regiment of mounted police galloping after him. Escape was hopeless, with a huge mob of cattle on his hands, and he sat down to wait. But suddenly the cavalry troop, black against the sun, wheeled off the ridge of the dune and away over a claypan. It was a flock of emus.

At a race meeting at Burketown, that ill-starred Tombstone of the old Gulf Country, a lady caught sight of him and nudged her companion: 'That's Captain Moonlight'. Redford, by then nearly sixty but still a giant of a man with a white beard a foot square, swept his cabbage-tree hat from his head in courtly style and corrected her: 'Not Moonlight, madam. Starlight'.

The cattle stations that were formed in far western Queensland in the early days always faced a problem of how, and where, to bring their cattle to market. After that first epic cattle drive of Redford's in 1870, they were not slow to try the same route and bring their cattle to Adelaide by the so-called 'Strzelecki Track'. But it was soon found that seasons such as Redford had enjoyed were rare along the Strzelecki and that, in most years, the track offered neither water nor grass over a long stretch that ended in a perfect horror of sandhills called the Cobblers.

In 1872 a hard-drinking Sydney man named Robert Frew had founded a town called Birdsville on the Diamantina River, just north of the border between South Australia and Queensland. He named it Birdsville because of the abundance of bird life that he discovered on the nearby permanent lagoons of the Diamantina.

Birdsville was not much of a town. At first, it consisted solely of the store that Frew had set up to supply the squatters who were just beginning to move into this area. But it so happened that Birdsville occupied a strategic position at the head of a possible cattle route to Adelaide that was better watered and more

above: **Burke and Wills Camp 76, Diamantina River, Birdsville**

below: **Sturt's Stony Desert**

direct than the Strzelecki Track which looped more than a hundred miles to the east of it.

The pioneer of this new stock route, the Birdsville Track, also established the record journey for the track. He was a head drover called Tom Ford who, in 1882, took control of a mob of 2 000 cattle from John Costello's Lake Nash Station, far up in the Northern Territory. He brought them down the Georgina River to Birdsville and then south-south-west, blazing out the route that was to become the Birdsville Track. Ford delivered the cattle in Adelaide after a drive of nine months and 1 500 miles.

This route was shortened when the railway line from Adelaide, 440 miles away, arrived at the town of Marree. This natural watering hole had been discovered by John McDouall Stuart's 1859 expedition and named Hergott Springs, for the Bavarian naturalist who accompanied Stuart's party. In 1883, it was proclaimed a government town, and re-named Marree (meaning 'place of many possums'). The railhead at Marree became the southern

terminus of the Birdsville Track and millions of head of cattle were railed from Marree to Adelaide over the years that the Birdsville Track operated as one of Australia's great cattle routes.

In the season between April and September some 50 000 head of cattle were driven down the Birdsville Track each year, and it was one of the epic sights of the inland to see the great herds of up to 2 000 cattle advancing across the plains, while behind them in clouds of dust rode the drovers, white and black, cracking their rawhide whips and colouring the dust a deeper red with their language.

The Birdsville Track has sometimes been compared with America's much glamorised Chisholm Trail. The reality is never likely to reach the millions who've been hypnotised by Hollywood but the fact is that, in terms of the guts and endurance needed to negotiate it, the Birdsville Track beats the Chisholm Trail into a cocked hat. (For that matter, the Australian term 'stockman' has always struck me as more impressive than the American term, 'cowboy'.

above: The ominous start of the Birdsville Track, Marree

below: Bore, Birdsville Track

What's a cowboy, after all, but a boy who's sent out to fetch the cows? As for the Australian term 'track' and the American 'trail', you can take your choice. I like 'track'.)

The Chisholm Trail was a mere 300 miles. The Birdsville Track was harder and it was longer. From Birdsville to Marree alone was 350 miles, but most of the cattle came twice as far as that, from Boulia in Queensland and from stations even further north. Birdsville was not the northern end of the track, but the central point. However, the cattle could be brought down on the first half of their journey by a number of routes through the Channel Country of south-west Queensland, which usually provided reasonable grass and water. Birdsville was the focal point where the mobs came together, because from there south there was only one possible stock route. And even that was far from being safe.

The Chisholm Trail was only once negotiated in extreme weather conditions. The Birdsville Track was attempted by the Queensland drovers year after year, in conditions that might have driven lesser men to suicide. Sometimes it almost amounted to suicide. Numbers of instances were recorded where drovers lost their entire mobs in the choking sandstorms north of the Cooper and narrowly escaped with their own lives. There were probably many more such instances that went unrecorded. It was that kind of country. But, for eighty years, the drovers brought their cattle down the track and regarded it all casually enough — just another job. In theory, the Birdsville Track followed a chain of waterholes, but for the first thirty years of the track the drovers could never be sure of finding water in those holes. They had to become very astute judges of the weather and it also helped a bit if they were born lucky.

At the beginning of the twentieth century, an artesian water reservoir was found to be under this apparently hopeless country. The South Australian Government sank a series of bores, which made pastoral settlement along the track possible, and also made conditions somewhat easier for the drovers. However, it was never *that* easy. The drovers could only shift their cattle about eight miles a day, and in drought seasons, when the natural waterholes were dry, they might face stretches of three days and more between bores. Feed for the cattle would be as scarce as hen's teeth, while blazing heat and dust storms stuck to them as faithfully as the flies.

On rarer occasions, they encountered the opposite natural extreme, flood. Such is the contrary nature of the Birdsville Track country that when floods do come, they come in such proportions as to make Noah throw up his hands and pull the plug out of his Ark. Drovers who'd mothered their cattle for hundreds of miles could see them borne away in a moment by a flash Cooper flood, bound for the briny waters of Lake Eyre.

Whatever the weather, the drover always had to undergo the penalties attendant on his trade. He was, to all appearances, a carefree customer and a king of men. Through the days, he rode to the soothing jingle of spurs and Condamine bells; at night, he saw the wondrous glory of the everlasting stars. What the envious townie didn't see was the other side of the drover's life — the heat, the thirst, the mortal risks, the hard ground for his bed, the basic rations, the long nights without sleep when the cattle were disturbed and inclined to rush (or, in American, stampede); and the biggest worry of all, the worry of bringing the cattle through alive.

But the people who lived in the cattle country knew about the darker side of the drover's dream. And the boss drovers who managed to bring their cattle through, year after year, in good condition and with few losses, became men of renown amongst the people whose opinion they most valued. It was, primarily, the exploits of those drovers that made the Birdsville Track what it is today in Australian legend — a by-word for endurance, courage and survival against the worst of natural odds.

The days of the great cattle drives down the Birdsville Track are over. Cattle are still occasionally brought by foot from the local stations to the Marree railhead — more often nowadays they're trucked in — but it's ten years since the last big mob came down on the hoof from Queensland. Nowadays the Queensland cattle are kept in prime condition and shipped to different destinations, in cattle trucks, along the new beef roads.

And yet the Birdsville Track retains its legendary reputation. In some ways, the reputation is no longer deserved. The original Track was for cattle. It was never designed for vehicles and until the 1960s, the so-called 'road' was just a pair of wheeltracks pioneered by August Helling's mail coach in the 1880s and gradually incised into the stony plains and the saltpans by the wheels of drovers' wagons, the station trucks, and the mail truck. In places like the sandhills north of the Cooper, the tracks often disappeared, covered by sand drift, and the traveller without local knowledge could find himself in big trouble.

All that has changed now, and the Birdsville Track is a graded country road, not much different from any other outback road. Some stretches have been re-routed by the South Australian Highways Department and the most notorious traps of the old days have been eliminated. It's still not what you'd call a fast road, but in normal weather, and without any stops, a conventional two-wheel drive car could expect to make the trip in twelve to fourteen hours — the same trip that took the old-time drovers a couple of months or more.

But it would be wrong, and dangerous, to think that either living on the Birdsville Track or travelling on it has become just a pushover. The area is populated, but only just. Less than eighty people live along the 350 miles between Marree and Birdsville and they are a pretty special breed of people. Life for them has never been easy, and never will be, in this semi-desert country where cattle stations are just marginally possible and profitable. In fact, they survive because nearly all of them belong, or are related by birth or marriage, to one family, the Oldfields, and their huge stations, of up to two thousand square miles, are run on a clan basis. There are no fences between the properties, and the cattle graze over vast areas. The station-owners admit that there are remote corners of their properties that they never see, and are never likely to.

The battle for survival has shaped the character and outlook of these people. They are tough, laconic, resourceful, big-hearted and given to quite remarkable understatement.

They don't have the civilised veneer of city folk, but they have developed a philosophy to cope with hardships and calamities that would drive city people mad. The old-style bush Australians are supposed to have disappeared under the twentieth century's tidal wave of soft living, labour-saving gadgets and television, but they haven't disappeared. They are alive and well and living on the Birdsville Track.

And the Track itself, like the people along it, has to be treated with respect. In good conditions it presents no problems for reliable vehicles; but the conditions aren't always good and some of the vehicles that have attempted the Track haven't been reliable.

In the cattle-droving days, the major traffic flowed south, from Birdsville down to the Marree railhead. Now, most of the traffic flows north from Marree, which is a much bigger town than Birdsville, and a less remote starting-point for tourists who want to experience the Birdsville Track. At Marree, motorists are asked to call at the Police Station for advice before attempting the Track. Not every motorist does this, but it's a good idea, and it could even mean the difference between life and death. At the Police Station they are first of all advised whether the Track is open. It sounds surprising, in such an arid country, but the Birdsville Track is sometimes closed by floods, when waters from faraway Queensland rain catchments surge down the Cooper and the Diamantina and swell those streams to immense proportions.

Even if the floods are negotiable, the motorist still needs to know whether he can get across the Cooper road crossing, or whether he will need to take a detour further upstream to the ferry that operates in flood times. And then he needs to know what to do at Clifton Hills Station, below the Diamantina, where the Track splits into two. In dry conditions, the Inside Track is the better and more direct route to Birdsville, but it traverses the Diamantina flood plains, and when the river is up, the Outside Track is the only way to Birdsville. At the other extreme of weather, in high summer, tourists are discouraged from attempting the Track at all. Anyone can suffer a mechanical breakdown; it's a long way between homesteads; and in the heat of January twelve hours is about as long as anyone could last out there without water.

Whatever the weather conditions, the Police Sergeant checks tyres, and petrol and water supplies. The station owners on the Track have petrol for their own uses but it's hard enough for them to keep up their supplies and they're not anxious to see their petrol drained away by passing motorists. The first petrol for sale after Marree is at Birdsville — and Birdsville has been known to run out of supplies. Ideally, the motorist is advised he should carry enough petrol, in spare tanks or jerry cans, to get him up to Birdsville *and* back to Marree. Say forty gallons; and he should also take an equal quantity of water.

Finally, the motorist is asked to go through the ritual of filling out two cards, stating his intended route, the make and colour and registration number of his vehicle, the names of his passengers and the date of travel. One of these cards is left at the Police Station at Marree; the other is to be handed in to the Police Station at Birdsville, on arrival. If he

doesn't arrive, at least the police will know he's missing, and know what to look for. The most important piece of advice on the card is this:

'If the vehicle breaks down or you become lost, *STAY* with it. A vehicle is much easier to find than a person on foot.'

Marree, a gaunt frontier town with a broad main street and a venerable two-storied hotel, the Great Northern, was an early headquarters of the Afghans, the camel-drivers brought out from the North-West Frontier of India by Sir Thomas Elder to look after the camels which he introduced to nearby Beltana Station in 1866. At Marree, they had their own settlement, 'Ghan Town' on the eastern side of the railway line, where they planted date palms around their houses and worshipped Allah in a mosque of corrugated iron. Some of their descendants still live in Marree, but the mosque and most other traces of 'Ghan Town' have vanished.

below: **Lake Harry Homestead**

These Afghans, resourceful bushmen and energetic traders, did much of the pioneering of the Birdsville Track. Walking out from Marree with their camels loaded with rations, machinery and fencing wire for the stations far to the north, they found many of the waterholes that became the drovers' rests along the track. The first of these can be seen half an hour's drive out of Marree — Lake Harry. It was formerly a government camel-breeding station and the stumps of date palms around the abandoned stone homestead recall the vanished Afghan camel-masters. Just past Lake Harry is the dog fence that was built through 5 000 miles of New South Wales, Queensland, South Australia and Western Australia to keep dingoes out of the sheep country.

Once you pass this fence you're in dingo country. And it soon becomes obvious that you're in cattle country. At Clayton River, the site of an early drovers' camp, Kevin Oldfield runs the most southern of the Oldfields' chain

of stations and he and his sons can quite likely be seen on the plains beside the road, herding cattle with their Suzukis and stockhorses. Kevin showed me the cattle pads worn into the plains by the vast mobs that came down from Queensland, and his sons, lolling casually on horseback, discoursed in their western drawls on the merits of Barcoo poley saddles, and the various brands of stockwhip.

Approaching Dulkaninna Station, which, with its pioneer homestead, has been held by the Bell family since the 1880s, blue lakes and ragged ranges can be seen shimmering in the distance. They are mirages. The first white man in this country was the South Australian Government Surveyor, Samuel Parry, in 1858. He named it 'The Plains of Illusion', and scattered around other names to suggest that it was a country where men were fated to be duped and disappointed — Mount Attraction, Mount Delusion, Decoy Hill.

Ten years later, a band of German Lutheran missionaries decided to ignore the warnings conveyed by Surveyor Parry's place-names. At Lake Killalpaninna, on the floodplains of the

below: **Ferry crossing, Cooper Creek**

lower Cooper as it flows towards Lake Eyre, they established a mission to preach the Gospel to the Dieri tribe. These prophets in the desert translated the Bible into Dieri dialect and they raised churches, schoolhouses, pastors' dwellings, harness sheds and sheep yards in this remote wilderness. Herman Vogelsang, the driving force of the mission, thundered a great sermon, based on the text from Ezekiel: 'And the desolate land shall be tilled and they shall say, "This, the land that was desolate, is become as the garden of Eden" '.

Perhaps, for a while, it seemed possible. The patriarch Vogelsang, with a sword in one hand and a Bible in the other, converted the Aborigines from warfare to hymn singing, and preached to them for nearly half a century. But the droughts were invincible and the mission was abandoned two years after Vogelsang's death in 1912. His grave, along with a couple of collapsed houses, the skeleton of a harness shed and the scattered remains of heavy German wagons, is all that remains of that lonely settlement beside the lake. Of the Dieri people, the subject of the Lutheran's long toil, nothing whatever remains.

A few other relics, collected from the settlement, have been preserved by Brian and Kath Oldfield at nearby Etadinna Station. In Vogelsang's day Etadinna was the mission's out-station and used to shear 30 000 sheep. Now it's a typical Birdsville Track cattle station and Brian and Kath Oldfield face the typical problems of these isolated stations — loneliness, long distances from shops of any kind, lack of communications. The children have to be sent far away to boarding school; even the nearest neighbour is far away, and Kath's usual contact with the other women on the Track is through their daily conversation on 'pedal wireless'. They still call it that, although the stations now have powerful transmitter/receivers that don't require pedalling; and the women's daily talk is referred to sardonically by the husbands as 'the galah session'.

Just north of Etadinna Station, the Birdsville Track crosses the Cooper and in past years you could usually drive straight across without getting your wheels wet. But the exceptional seasons of the last four years have kept the Cooper running down to Lake Eyre, and, even more remarkably, have kept Lake Eyre full to the brim. When I arrived at the Cooper Crossing, the water was a mile wide. It was necessary to detour upstream to the temporary ferry. This operates at one of the few points where the lower Cooper flows within clearly defined banks. Even there it looked as broad as the Murray, was flowing twenty feet deep, and was chock-full of big fat yellowbelly, or callop, which a few fishermen were catching with ridiculous ease.

The Cooper Ferry is a pretty quaint affair, driven along by two tiny outboard motors and operated by a man called, of all things, Cooper. The ferry is more intended for station stock than for people but it carries passenger vehicles, one at a time. There are strict rules: you have to get out of your vehicle and you have to strap on a life jacket. Apparently, a man sitting inside his truck was tipped off the ferry and drowned some years ago.

North of the Cooper are the Natarannie Sandhills, uninviting enough now, but really dreaded in the days before the new road. The track used to disappear completely under sand drifts and the mailman could only get his truck through by lugging steel boiler plates around to put under his wheels. He'd advance a few feet, then get out and do the whole thing again. Not surprisingly, the old Birdsville mail service was not always punctual, but it got there and it carried the heavy goods the station people wanted. They are still very hostile about the cancellation of the road mail a couple of years ago and its replacement by a fortnightly light plane service.

At Mulka, which has the lowest annual rainfall in Australia, a crumbling ruin stands beside the wheel ruts of the original Birdsville Track. This was once a bush store, kept by a Mrs Aiston, the widow of an outback policeman. Mrs Aiston lived alone, in what was possibly the loneliest store in the world. She was lucky if she saw one customer in a fortnight. Still, as she once said, 'when they came, they generally bought more than a pound of flour'. It was the only shop of any kind between Birdsville and Marree, and Mrs Aiston stocked the kind of things that drovers wanted — bridles and blankets, boots and saddles, pack needles and thread, quartpots and Bedourie camp ovens, waterbags and tucker. Now there is no shop at all between Birdsville and Marree, and all that is left at the old Mulka store is a couple of tottering walls and a lonely grave on the hillside out the back.

At Mungerannie Station, owned by Kevin Oldfield of Clayton River, another road branches west from the present Birdsville Track and runs out to Cowarie Station. The original Birdsville Track ran right past the front door of this station. In fact, the fine sandstone homestead and barn were built by the first Birdsville mailman, August Helling, nearly a century ago. Later, Cowarie belonged to Sydney Kidman. Now, it's owned by yet another Oldfield, Claude.

With his hat tipped back from his forehead, and a rolled cigarette hanging from his bottom lip, Claude can tell you the driest stories imaginable; but, on his horse, galloping full pelt around the yards and roping cattle, he looks a hard-bitten customer. He'd need to be, to live in this country. Across the Warburton, or lower Diamantina, from Cowarie, the Simpson Desert begins. This is the last possible limit of cattle country. Drought is the usual problem, but floods have also taken their toll of Cowarie from time to time, inundating huge areas of the 2 000 square mile station, and bogging or marooning thousands of head of cattle. The Oldfields have lasted out on Cowarie for thirty-eight years without going broke, but Claude admits that it hasn't been easy.

At Clifton Hills, a desolate homestead on the gibber plains, the road divides into the Inside and Outside Track, and if the Diamantina's up, there's only one choice, the Outside Track. This track leads through some of the most forbidding landscape on this planet. The whole area looks as if it's been paved with shimmering caramel-coated rock. It was here that Sturt wrote in his journal: 'It is a country such as I firmly believe has no parallel on earth's surface! Other deserts there are, but they present not the steel-shod appearances of this desperate region. We are as lonely as a ship at sea or a navigator seeking land.'

It was so hot that the bolts were squeezed from his bullock cart, the lead dropped out of his pencils, and sunstruck birds fell dead from the sky. It was all a ghastly mockery of the scene he had hoped to find, the Inland Sea where he would sail his whaleboat and display the British flag. Yet he sensed, correctly, that his dream had not been entirely ridiculous; that there were signs here of a long-ago sea:

'The appearance of the Desert was like that of an immense sea beach, and large fragments of rock were imbedded in the ground, as if by the force of waters, and the stones were more scattered, thus showing the sandy bed beneath and betwixt them. The day was exceeding hot and our horses' hoofs were so brittle that pieces flew off them like splinters when they struck them against the stones.'

With that agonising image, and pausing only to name a watercourse for his friend, Judge Cooper of Adelaide, Sturt bade adieu to the repellent region that now bears his name — Sturt's Stony Desert.

The Outside Track continues north into great lines of sand dunes, as eerie as the stony plain and, for some travellers, more deadly. Upwards of fifty dead travellers — stockmen, drovers, swagmen, mystery men — have been found in the Cooper and Diamantina sandhills, and some are buried there. The bush poet, Barcroft Boake, must have had country like this in mind when he wrote, before hanging himself with his own stockwhip:

'Out on the wastes of the Never Never
That's where the dead men lie!
There where the heat-waves dance for ever
That's where the dead men lie!'

Deadman Sandhill, beside the Outside Track, gained its name at the turn of the century, when three stockmen got bushed there as they were riding back to their station from the Birdsville races. Apparently they were without water and crazed from sunstroke and Birdsville grog. Two of their horses ran away and they ended up cutting the third horse's throat to drink his blood. But that couldn't save them and they all perished — which means, in outback language, that they died of dehydration.

As recently as 1963, Deadman Sandhill proved that it deserved its name and the

Birdsville Track proved that it was still not to be trifled with. An English migrant family, the Pages, disregarding advice not to attempt the Track in a heatwave, drove up from Marree and on Christmas Eve their car ran out of petrol at Deadman Sandhill. There was still water in the car radiator, but the Pages set out to walk for help and were hopelessly bushed in temperatures over the century. A week later, the blackened and shrivelled bodies of Ernest Page, his wife and their three sons, were found under a coolabah tree and buried near Deadman Sandhill.

The Pages had broken every rule in the book. They travelled at the wrong time, they didn't tell anyone where they were going, they didn't carry enough petrol or enough water and they didn't stay with their car. On the little-frequented Outside Track, anyone who broke all those rules today would be likely to come to the same fate as the Pages.

Past George Morton's Pandie Pandie Station is the border gate to Queensland and then the Diamantina River and journey's end — Birdsville. It's no great metropolis — the population is about sixty — but it's a welcome sight to the traveller. The first pub, the first store, the first street, the first village of any kind in over 300 miles.

Civilisation does show some signs of advancing on Birdsville at an unexpected rate. It now has a pedestrian crossing and an angle parking sign, and it is linked to the world by radio-telephone. But it's still an outback Queensland town, and even if the great cattle mobs no longer pass through, it still has its peculiar claims to fame.

Correct behaviour in Birdsville is first to hand in your travel card to the policeman — a hard working fellow with a beat of 35 000 square miles — and then to proceed to the pub to wash the dust of the Birdsville Track out of your throat. When I did this, the publican informed me that I'd just missed the event of the year, the Birdsville Races. It had been a great turn, and the pub had got away 'eighty of beer'. Since the only beer available was in cans or stubbies, I ventured that he meant eighty crates. 'Wrong,' he grinned. *'Eighty tons!'* I can only say that a place with a thirst like that has to be 'The Real Outback'.

below: **The Birdsville Hotel**

opposite: **Mount Conner, Central Australia**

THE CENTRE

The centre of every continent has been penetrated but that of Australia. Thousands of pounds have been expended in expeditions to the Poles, but this country, round which a girdle of civilisation is forming, is neglected, and its recesses, whether desert or fertile, are unexplored.

'Over the centre of this mighty continent there hangs a veil which the most ambitious would be proud to raise.'

Those were the words of the explorer, Charles Sturt, in Adelaide, April 1840. Five years later he might have been prepared to eat those words. He had by then raised the corner of the veil and was horrified by what he'd seen under it. The centre of the continent, or as near as he'd been able to penetrate towards it, had not revealed the Inland Sea of his dreams, but instead a hellish inferno of stony wastes and sandy deserts, a region that appeared to be a creation of Satan rather than of God. But Sturt, for all his efforts, was still far from the true centre of Australia. So were Burke and Wills, in their fatal expedition of 1860. The centre was still hundreds of miles west of their tracks and the honour of raising the veil was to fall to an indomitable little Scot, John McDouall Stuart.

An earlier explorer, Edward John Eyre, had already tried twice to reach the centre of Australia by what seemed the most logical and direct way, striking due north of Adelaide. On his first attempt in 1839, he found his way blocked by the saltpan, Lake Torrens. The next year he tried again and it was in giving his blessing to Eyre's 1840 expedition that Sturt made his remarks about lifting the veil over the centre of the continent. But Eyre, like Sturt, was not destined to lift that veil. Striking north from the head of Port Augusta he came again to an apparently impenetrable barrier of saltpans. He endowed the name 'Mount Hopeless' on a nearby prominence to signify his decision to 'waste no more time or energy in so desolate and forbidding a region'.

Eyre had in fact reached the southern shore of the huge saltpan which is the residual sump of the ancient Central Sea (and which G. W. Goyder named for him, twenty years later,

'Lake Eyre'). But Eyre *thought* he had found a continuation of Lake Torrens and so he concluded that there was a great 'Horseshoe Lake' curving across the north of South Australia and forming an impassable barrier to further exploration.

This 'Horseshoe Lake' myth was not exploded for nearly twenty years, and it was because he believed in the 'Horseshoe Lake' that Sturt, in 1844, disregarded an official suggestion that he should strike north from Port Augusta towards the centre of the continent, and instead attempted his lateral assault, heading north-west from Menindee on the Darling. The draughtsman Sturt took with him on that journey of disappointment, was a thirty-year-old Scot, John McDouall Stuart. Stuart not only gathered valuable experience from that mission, but burned from then on with the zeal to make some great exploration on his own behalf.

By 1859 several explorers had established that the 'Horseshoe Lake' theory was wrong, and that paths to the north could be found between the saltpans. In that year Stuart made two trips north, discovering Hergott Springs (later Marree), exploring the western shores of Lake Eyre and finding tracts of promising country covered with grass and saltbush. In 1860, with two companions, Stuart launched the first of three attempts to cross the continent from south to north. He was not to achieve the distinction of being the first explorer to do it — that was to fall to Burke and Wills — but, in every other way, Stuart was more successful than that unfortunate pair.

Stuart passed through the MacDonnell Ranges and on April 22, 1860, made camp at a point that he calculated was the centre of the Australian continent. Choosing the nearest feature, which was a mountain a couple of miles to the north-east, Stuart ascended it, named it Central Mount Stuart, raised the British flag on its summit and called on his companions to give 'three cheers for Captain Sturt, the father of Australian exploration — and one more for Mrs Sturt and family!'.

Stuart pushed on north as far as Attack Creek, where, with food and water running low and under a state of seige from the Aborigines, he decided to return south. Stuart was back in

Adelaide by October, 1860, and one month later, with a bigger and better party, he was on his way north again. On this occasion, he reached Newcastle Waters before he was beaten back by dense scrub and shortage of rations. When Stuart returned to Adelaide in September, 1861, it was after a journey of ten months and privations that few men would wish to face again. But the irrepressible Stuart again allowed himself only one month for recuperation before launching his third attempt at the continental crossing. And this time he succeeded, reaching the northern seas at Chambers Bay, just east of the mouth of the Adelaide River, on July 24, 1862.

The trip back was the hardest he ever made. Some of the horses had to be abandoned, Stuart himself became so weak that he had to be carried on a stretcher, and he recorded in his diary that he was reduced to 'a perfect skeleton'. Honours were showered upon him on his return to Adelaide — money, gold medals, rent-free leases of land in the north — but Stuart didn't live long enough to enjoy them. He was a hard-living, hard-driving, hard-drinking man, and he had demanded too much of the human body. His eyesight and his memory progressively failed and he died at the age of fifty, less than four years after completing his last great expedition.

Such honours as he had received were richly deserved. Stuart had absolutely refused to give up. Unlike the two explorers who beat him to the north coast, but lost their lives, Stuart never lost a man on any of his expeditions. And he had crossed squarely through the centre of Australia and unselfishly named its central feature for that great explorer who'd hoped to do the same, Charles Sturt.

But the names Sturt and Stuart were distinguished by only a single letter, and by one of those little accidents that sometimes correct the injustices of history, a clerk in Adelaide transcribed on to the maps the name of that central mountain as 'Central Mount Stuart', not 'Central Mount Sturt'. Central Mount Stuart has been its name ever since, and so it should be. Nobody deserves this memorial more than the little man who proved, once and for all, that there was no lush inland sea rippling in the centre of the

continent, but that there were, instead, vast tracts of land that could be put to some use.

Giles, Gosse, Warburton and a whole posse of explorers followed Stuart into the Centre and to look at a map of the tangled tracks they pursued is enough to set the head spinning; but the most tangible, and the most important consequence of Stuart's epic journey was the construction of the Overland Telegraph Line.

Completed in 1872, the Overland Telegraph Line, stretching 1 800 miles from Port Augusta to Port Darwin (or 'Palmerston') was one of the greatest developments in Australian communications. It was the first telegraphic system to span Australia from coast to coast, and it was the first link to join Australia, via Java, to the telegraphic networks of Asia and Europe. Previously, Australia was forced to rely on the monthly mail services of the P&O shipping line for its communications with Europe. The first cable was transmitted by the Overland Telegraph Line in 1872 and it was then, as Charles Heavitree Todd, Postmaster-General of South Australia, expressed it, that 'the Australian Colonies were connected with the grand electric chain which unites all the nations of the earth'.

In planning the line, especially its central sections, the surveyors relied heavily on the journals of John McDouall Stuart. But at one point in the centre they deviated from Stuart's south-to-north corridor. His route through the MacDonnell Ranges was not suitable for the construction of the line and the surveyor, John Ross, chose instead a pass thirty five miles further east. This pass became known as Heavitree Gap, after the middle name of the Postmaster-General who was credited with the instigation of the Overland Telegraph Line. The river running through the Gap, the Todd, was also named for him while the locality of the telegraph station, established on springs a few miles north, was named Alice Springs in honour of Todd's wife, Alice.

Between these two Toddish monuments a tiny settlement began and it was called Stuart, which was only fair. Stuart had seen a good deal more of this country than had Charles Todd or his wife Alice. But the name, Alice Springs, caught the popular imagination, perhaps because it sounded prettier than

above: Ancient paintings, ancient rocks

Stuart, and eventually the name of the town was officially changed to Alice Springs. Unofficially, Territorians called the place 'The Alice', or just 'Alice'.

Alice Springs is now part of the Northern Territory, but it enjoyed a brief spell of glory from 1926 to 1931 as the administrative capital of a separate territory called Central Australia. The old Administration Building still stands in the town. Central Australia was actually the southern half of the Northern Territory. The border was drawn along the 20th Parallel, just below Tennant Creek. But the official territory of Central Australia was never much more than a state of mind. In 1931, with the onset of the Depression, Central Australia was abolished to save the cost of supporting an administration in Alice Springs and it became once again a part of the Northern Territory, administered from Darwin.

In any case, the official status of Alice Springs, as capital of Central Australia, had sounded misleadingly grand. The reality was much humbler. In the early 1920s there were only about fifty white residents in the town.

There were more Aborigines but they weren't counted. In 1927 the report of the first Government resident, Cawood, stated the entire population of Central Australia as 411 — a pretty meagre figure for an area of a quarter of a million square miles, three times bigger than Britain. In 1928, he reported that the white population had fallen to 400, but this time he added that there were 5 500 Aborigines and half-castes in Central Australia.

The event that really kicked Alice Springs along was the arrival of the railway from Adelaide in 1929. The regular train was called the 'Ghan', in tribute to the Afghan camel-drivers who'd previously fetched the supplies to the town. Alice Springs became the railhead for the big cattle stations that had been established in the Centre, and its population began to grow. The population was further increased in 1932, when the Ghan brought up crowds of miners, prospectors and adventurers, all bound for a new goldfield at

The Granites, which was in the Tanami Desert, hundreds of miles north-west of Alice Springs.

Cloudy Beale, one of the old-time residents of Alice Springs, arrived on the Ghan just before The Granites goldrush. Cloudy (she was given that name because she smoked a lot of cigarettes and was generally seen approaching in a cloud of smoke) recalls that the streets when she arrived were full of stockmen in bright blue shirts and ten-gallon hats and jingling spurs, and that their casual shouts of greeting to all and sundry, 'Good day, mate!' and 'Hi ya, Missus!' struck her, a lady fresh from the city, as rather too familiar and presumptuous. She was appointed postmistress at Ryan's Well, on the track between Alice Springs and The Granites, and she saw the gold-seekers on their way out, full of hope, and she saw them come back, beaten and half-starved. The Granites goldrush was a terrible disappointment but it was one of many mineral rushes that helped to swell the population of the Centre.

Gold was mined at Arltunga, east of Alice Springs, as early as the 1880s, and a substantial mining town was built there. It's now deserted, but many of the buildings remain. In more recent times, mica has been mined at Hart's Range and gold at Tennant Creek. Even at Tanami, just north of The Granites, substantial quantities of gold were recovered after World War Two, though that was no consolation to the men who'd gone bust out there in the 1930s.

Mining was one of the two industries that helped to develop the land that Stuart had thrown open in the centre of Australia. The other was grazing. Very large cattle-stations were formed, each of 1 000 to 2 000 square miles, and by the early 1950s, some 40 000 head of cattle were being trucked by rail from Alice Springs to Adelaide each year.

But although the Centre has proved to be reasonable cattle country, it is not great cattle country. Australia has many areas that are better suited to raising cattle. Good rainfall is not unknown in the Centre — it has enjoyed good seasons for each of the past five years — but the average rainfall is low and in the late 1950s and early 1960s the whole country suffered a hideous drought.

The safe cattle-carrying capacity of the Centre is not high but graziers have not always resisted the temptation to overstock in good years with resultant damage to the country. In the Centre, as in other arid regions, there is a delicate natural balance between soil, herbage and rainfall. Overgrazing is the quickest way to destroy that balance, kill the natural regeneration of the grass cover, and turn the country into a wilderness of erosion and dust-storms. Perhaps some of the past mistakes were understandable (although there's not much excuse now), because the Centre can often look to be better grazing country than it really is. The natural regenerative powers of the soil are enormous and countless people have remarked on the miracle of the Centre after rain, when grass and vivid wildflowers spring from the earth in profusion.

Then, as they say, 'the desert blooms', an inaccurate observation because most of the Centre isn't desert. But it's not the first inaccurate observation that we've made about the Centre. The farming and grazing outlook has been embedded deep in the Australian mentality from early times. The prime motive of the explorers, and the men who financed them, was to open up new lands for farming and grazing. It has taken us a long time to conclude that some of our continent is better left unploughed and ungrazed and undisturbed; that it may be wiser, and indeed may be more profitable, just to leave it alone and look at it. That is what is happening in the Centre now, and it represents the wave of the future for that country. Anyone who doesn't believe that a community can support itself just by taking people around and showing them things ought to visit Alice Springs today. It's grown a bit since the days of the little struggletown called Stuart.

Alice now has some 14 000 people. Although it's a thousand miles from the nearest capital city, it's booming and practically the entire basis of the boom is tourism — people coming to look at things and spend a bit of money on their way. Alice Springs itself is not such a remarkable town to look at but its situation, and the natural marvels that lie all around it, are likely to guarantee its future for longer than the cattle industry could.

One interesting example of how tourism has altered the traditional occupations of the Centre can be seen at Ross River, east of Alice Springs in the MacDonnell Ranges. For many years, the holding formed part of Love's Creek Station, which was run by the pioneering Bloomfield family, who bred horses for the Indian remount trade. When that trade collapsed, the Bloomfields switched to cattle but they lost 8 000 head in the drought of the late 1950 s and were practically wiped out.

The brothers, Gil and Doug Green, were in the area at that time, cutting redgum sleepers for the Commonwealth Railways. They were struck by the natural beauty of the place, leased the homestead block from the Bloomfields and set about restoring the pioneer homestead which had lost its roof and doors. Next to the homestead they built a group of simple timber cabins. Today, the Green brothers operate the place as the Ross River Resort and it is one of the most popular tourist attractions in the Centre. They have worked very hard to preserve the atmosphere of a traditional Australian station homestead, avoiding anything garish or incongruous, and they get thousands of visitors from Australia and overseas who are looking for a taste of the old-style bush life.

At Ross River, the tourists can ride horses through the beautiful scenery of the river and the ranges, go on picnics offering barbecued steaks and damper and billy tea and traditional bush yarns from the brothers Green, and take excursions to nearby points of interest — Arltunga ghost-town, Trephina Gorge and the Valley of the Eagles.

These natural features are east of Alice Springs and there is even more to see west of Alice. It may not have been the same Alice that Lewis Carroll had in mind but Australia's Alice *is* in Wonderland, surrounded on all sides by marvels of nature that stagger the imagination.

The most famous of them is indisputably Ayers Rock. It is the one thing that every visitor from overseas has heard about and that every tourist wants to see. Sixty thousand

top: **Wildflowers, the Centre**

left: **The desert blooms**

tourists a year have been arriving to inspect the Rock by road or by air — it's a couple of hours' flight south-west from Alice Springs. Many of them stop over in the tourist motels at the base of the Rock and there are forecasts that tourist traffic could rise to the daunting figure of 60 000 a *week*. Yet it had very few white visitors until 1930 and it was only as recently as 1950 that the first organised party of tourists was taken to the Rock.

Ayers Rock was sighted by the explorer, William Gosse, in 1873 and named for the Premier of South Australia, Sir Henry Ayers. Although it is sometimes called the world's biggest boulder, it is in fact a mountain peak — one of the three visible peaks of a buried mountain range that once stretched from east to west across Central Australia.

Ayers Rock is immensely old — at least 500 million years — immensely huge and spectacularly red. This great block of

right: **A rare sight, the river flows**

below: **Claw marks of Kulpunya, Ayers Rock**

sandstone, over 1 000 feet high and five miles round, sculpted by the erosion of the long centuries and by the local storms which its own mass creates, is one of the world's most stunning spectacles. Tourists expend large amounts of energy climbing it by a man-made trail, and large amounts of film capturing its moods and colours from the photographer's vantage point called 'Sunset Strip'. Yet many of them leave Ayers Rock unaware of its rich legendary associations and its central place in the long human history of Australia that preceded the white man's history.

When John McDouall Stuart hoisted the British flag at the centre of Australia, he saw it as 'a sign to the natives that the dawn of liberty, civilisation, and Christianity is about to break upon them'. It was a horribly mistaken prophecy. The white man's coming represented not the dawn, but the twilight for the Aboriginal nations. But Stuart's statement was typical of the Australian explorers. They were diverse in their personalities, skills and achievements, but in their general approach to cultural questions they were, almost to a man, British Christian imperialists of the most simple-minded variety.

Only Captain Cook, a man of exceptionally broad vision and sympathies, had recognised that the Aborigines already enjoyed a way of life ideally suited to their needs, and that they were unlikely to appreciate or benefit from the introduction of white civilisation. And even Cook never realised that these apparently primitive people had arrived at their own explanations of the origins and meaning of life, and had created in their Dreamtime legends a tapestry of myth and religion as rich as Christianity itself.

For the tribes of Central Australia, Ayers Rock was a keystone of their religious belief, and a most sacred place. They came on pilgrimages of hundreds of miles to hold their ritual ceremonies there. They called it 'Uluru', or 'the earth mother' — an ancient tribesman called Paddy Uluru, who lives at Ayers Rock, is still recognised as the ritual keeper of the rock. A waterhole on top of Ayers Rock was, the Aborigines believed, the abode of the Rainbow Serpent, one of the great creative spirits who had emerged from beneath the earth

at the dawn of time and created the natural features in a landscape that was previously quite flat and dead.

Every feature of the Rock had an explanation in their legends. Modern tourists have attached banal names to some of these places — the Bell, Napoleon's Hat, the Brain — but the Aboriginal explanations are more imaginative and more interesting. For instance, the Brain, a huge eroded scar pattern on the north face of the Rock, has been given that name by white men because it resembles the shape and the involuted surface of an exposed human brain. But, to the Aborigines, these scars were the traces of a great battle that took place in the Dreamtime. The battle arose out of a disagreement between the Windulka, or Mulga Seed Men, of the Petermann Ranges, and the Mala, or Hare Wallaby People, at Ayers Rock.

The Mulga Seed Men had invited the Mala to their initiation ceremonies, but the Mala sent back word that they were not interested — they were too busy with their own ceremonies. Incensed at this discourtesy, the Mulga Seed Men had their witchdoctors create a malignant being to destroy the Mala. These medicine men assembled a skeletal frame of Mulga branches and women's hair and marsupial teeth and a bandicoot's tail. They breathed life into it with their songs of magic, and it became a giant murderous dingo, Kulpunya. They sent this Dreamtime Frankenstein's monster slouching eastward over the plains to teach the Mala a lesson.

The Mala, or Hare Wallaby People, huddled in caves high on the face of the rock, but Kulpunya swarmed straight up the side to attack them. The holes that can be seen ascending the north face, two by two, are the marks gouged by Kulpunya's claws. The brain-like formations at the top are the scars he left as he dug into the caves to seize his victims and eat them.

West of Ayers Rock lies another amazing spectacle — an improbable rock formation which was found by Ernest Giles in 1872 and given the suitably improbable name of Mount Olga, in honour of the Queen of Spain. Giles wrote:

'The appearance of this mountain is marvellous in the extreme, and baffles accurate description . . . it displayed to our astonished eyes rounded minarets, giant cupolas, and monstrous domes. I can only liken Mount Olga to several enormous rotund or rather elliptical shapes . . . which had been placed beside one another by some extraordinary freak or convulsion of Nature.'

It was, as Giles said, not one but a series of peaks, and nowadays it is called The Olgas. The Aborigines, as usual, had a more meaningful name for it. They called it Katijuta, meaning 'many heads' and in their lore it was a sacred fortress of the spirit people. For instance, it was the haunt of Pungalunga, a giant who strode about the plains with the corpses of old man kangaroos dangling from his belt. So remote are the Olgas, and so fantastic are its fortresses like the Valley of the Winds, that even now it is not difficult to sense the presence of that spirit world that awed the ancient tribes.

Sturt and the other early explorers who postulated the presence of an Inland Sea were right in their instincts, even if they were wrong in their dates. Central Australia has been a marine land at several periods of the earth's history. A hundred million years ago, it was the bed of an ocean strait that divided the western continent, Yilgarnia, from the chain of islands that became the eastern continent.

A million years ago, Central Australia was still an inland swamp, lush, steamy and subtropical. Incredibly, part of that ancient world is still preserved at Palm Valley. In this unique oasis, the tall cliffs shelter beautiful stands of the Livistona Mariae palm, a direct descendant from that world where diprotodons and giant kangaroos grazed on the swampy shores of the central waters. Somehow, they have survived the climatic changes which transformed the rest of the Centre into a region of arid plains and saltpans and rock outcrops of vivid red.

The first tourists reached Palm Valley in the 1920s, negotiating the last twelve miles from Hermannsburg Mission by camel. Now, it's another of the spectacles that draw tourists in droves to Central Australia. There are so many magnificent spectacles in the Centre, so many breathtaking mountains and amphitheatres and gorges, that superlatives soon fail.

But each has something different to show. King's Canyon, with walls so sheer that they might have been carved by the axe of the giant Pungalunga, is the biggest gorge in the Centre. Standley Chasm, named for Mrs Ida Standley, Alice Springs' first schoolteacher, is the narrowest gorge, so narrow that it's only lit by sunshine for ten minutes of the day, just after noon. Gosse's Bluff, a ring of mountains, was once considered to be the result of a geological fluke. Now it's thought to be a meteorite crater, the biggest in the world.

And then there are Glen Helen Gorge, Ormiston Gorge, Simpson's Gap — the list of supercolossal spectaculars rolls on like the productions of Cecil B. de Mille. But, for sheer grandeur, the palm must go to the Big Three, which are the three peaks of the buried Central Australian Range. Each is visible from the other and they stand across the country, in a direct line from east to west, like three giant sentries at their posts. Mount Olga is the western peak, Ayers Rock is the central peak, and Mount Conner is the eastern peak. Mount Conner, a great mass of quartzite whose flat top is covered with spinifex and eucalypts, is the least-remarked of the three giant monoliths, but it has its own interest.

In Aboriginal lore, Mount Conner was the ancient camp of the most fearsome of all mythical beings, the Ninya, or Ice Men. The Ninya are the spirits of winter and frost. In summer they live underground in vast caverns of perpetual cold, but in winter they emerge to stalk about the landscape, their bodies white with frost and their beards and eyebrows masses of tinkling icicles. The ice and frost that fall from their bodies freeze the grass and the waterholes, while the howling winds that always accompany them bring the chill of winter to the Centre.

The main significance of Mount Conner for white tourists is that they often mistake it, at first sight, for Ayers Rock. But then, mistakes are nothing new in the Centre. From the first confusion that turned Central Mount Sturt into Central Mount Stuart, through a century

of attempts to graze sheep and cattle in land that couldn't take it, and right up to the present time, we have mistaken the limitations and possibilities of the Centre, and we have looked at the country without really seeing it.

Only now are we coming to realise what the Aborigines knew for tens of thousands of years. The Centre is not the kind of country that can serve any purpose we require of it; it has to be accepted on its own terms. We can either ruin it, or take it as it is. And since Nature has casually left lying around in that country some of the most wonderful scenery in the world, it shouldn't be too hard for us to take it as it is.

above: **Brief sunshine in Standley Chasm, just after noon**

opposite: **Pandanus swamp, Arnhem Land**

Central Australia is a country that was made to be looked at. Provided — and it's an important provision — that the tourist industry is handled so as to avoid disfiguring scenic places with inappropriate buildings, then we can keep the country unharmed as the Aborigines did; the world will always have this wonderland and tourism will provide a lively future for what has sometimes been called, wrongly, 'The Dead Heart of Australia'.

ARNHEM LAND

Nobody could ever write the complete history of Australia, that is, the story of everything that ever happened in Australia. Even if they could write it, nobody would have lifetime or patience enough to read it. Any work of history is necessarily a selection of events, but granted that and granted that Australian historians select different events and interpret them in different ways, there is still a dimension lacking in the history that most of us learn. It is a white man's version of history, written from the point of view of a race that first encountered the Australian continent less than five centuries ago, and has occupied the continent for less than two centuries.

The black Australians, who have lived in the country two hundred times longer than the white Australians, have their own ideas about the history of Australia. At one time there were three hundred distinct Aboriginal languages and one could probably say that there were three hundred distinct Aboriginal versions of history. Conventional white historians would not have called any of it history. They'd have called it myth, legend or just plain fairy tales. It was not written down; it gave no dates; it concerned itself with implausible spirits, and with animals wielding human and even divine powers; and it was totally unscientific in its explanations of human and natural phenomena.

But it *was* history and it still is, where it survives in tribal Aboriginal societies. It is history in the same sense as the Bible is history. It is a religious explanation of man's past (as well as his present and future) and whether or not we choose to take it literally, it throws light on a mysterious era in the development of the human race.

It was not recorded in the European style, by being written down in words, but it was nevertheless recorded by the Aborigines in their art, in their works and in their stories, songs, dances and rituals handed down through countless generations. One wonders how much we would be able to tell now of the history of ancient Greece and Rome if we had no written works by Herodotus or Livy or Tacitus, but only memories passed on orally through centuries of ancestors.

In Australia, the earliest white man's history and the earliest black man's history both began in the same place, on the northern coast. But, in terms of their experiences and the way they interpreted those experiences, they might have been on different planets.

Consider first the white man's history. Willem Jansz, a Dutchman in the employ of the Dutch East India Company, was the first white man to arrive at the Australian coast. Jansz sailed from Bantam, Java, in the *Duyfken*, along the southern coast of New Guinea and then south-east into the Gulf of Carpentaria. In March, 1606, he sighted the west coast of Cape York in the vicinity of Pennefether River. He sailed southwards down this coast to a point he named Cabo Keerweer (Cape Turnagain). It is possible, I think, to detect a trace of disgust in that name. Jansz saw nothing but apparently barren coast. When he sent a boat ashore, at least one of his men was killed by hostile blacks. The only verdict recorded on his trip to this territory was that he found 'no good to be done there'.

Seventeen years later, the Dutch came back to the Gulf of Carpentaria in two ships, the *Pera* and the *Arnhem*. Jan Carstenz, the skipper of the *Pera*, gave the region the name 'Carpentaria' in honour of Pieter de Carpentier, the Governor-General of the Dutch East Indies. He sailed for fourteen days along the Cape York coast towards the southern end of the Gulf and landed at the Staten River where, he recorded 'we have had a wooden column, in the absence of stone, nailed to a tree, there being carved thereon the following words: "In the year 1623 on 24 April there came two ships sent by the High and Mighty States-General." ' Carstenz fought several battles with the Aborigines and managed to capture one whom he took back with him to Batavia. There is no record of this Aborigine's fate, but it is to be doubted whether he made much impression on the High and Mighty States-General.

Carstenz, in his journal, made it clear that he was unimpressed by either the land or its people. He wrote: 'We have not seen one fruit-bearing tree, nor anything that man could make use of; there are no mountains or even hills . . . this is the most arid and barren region that could be found anywhere on the earth; the inhabitants too are the most wretched and poorest creatures that I have seen.'

The *Arnhem,* commanded by Willem van Colster, became separated from the *Pera* and, sailing westward across the Gulf of Carpentaria, discovered the north-eastern coast of the vast promontory that was later named for this ship, Arnhem Land. Skipper van Colster didn't linger long in the area which he called De Caep Hollandia (now Cape Arnhem), but sailed through the Wessel Islands and into the Arafura Sea, heading north-west for Banda.

Succeeding investigations of the Arnhem Land coast by Pieter Pieterszoon in 1636 and Abel Tasman in 1644 added some more Dutch place-names to the map, but did nothing to change Dutch opinions of the region or its inhabitants. Tasman charted a vast stretch of the northern Australian coastline but he did not find what Governor-General van Diemen had sent him to look for — a passage into the Pacific between the Southland (or 'New Holland' as they now called it) and New Guinea. A map drawn up by the Dutch East India Company after Tasman's voyage showed Australia and New Guinea joined by land.

Had Tasman found the passage through Torres Strait and come down the fertile east coast of Australia, the Dutch might well have changed their minds about this country and a New Amsterdam, rather than a Botany Bay, might have become the first white settlement. However, as it turned out, Tasman's journey was a great disappointment to all concerned. His report on Arnhem Land and the adjoining coastline has not survived but it is apparent from the Dutch East India Company's correspondence that everybody's worst impressions had been once again confirmed. The Dutch were now convinced that New Holland offered no prospects for trade but was a barren waste, populated by barbarous, poor and brutal nations.

The Dutch abandoned further exploration of New Holland for trade purposes. There was, however, an interesting minute by the directors of the Dutch East India Company which hinted at a slight premonition, the merest of inklings, that they might have missed something. The minute said that it would probably be better now if that mysterious country to the south should remain forever mysterious and unexplored, lest something might be discovered there that could lead to the destruction of the company.

But Governor-General van Diemen had been in his grave for a century and a half before other white men, British men, discovered a useful purpose in the mysterious southern continent. And although the Dutch objected to the British occupation of Australia and claimed sovereignty by right of their earlier discovery of the continent, they had made no attempt to colonise the country themselves. The British, calculating that possession was ten points of the law, ignored the Dutch protests.

In 1802, Captain Matthew Flinders sailed from Port Jackson in the *Investigator* to explore the northern coastline of Australia. He had with him a copy of the Dutch map drawn up after Tasman's voyage, and after he'd sailed through Torres Strait into the Gulf of Carpentaria he did his best to identify and name the places indicated on the Dutch chart. But when he came to the area of the cape first sighted by van Colster in 1623 (and which Flinders now named 'Cape Arnhem') he found this land no kinder to him than it had been to the Dutch.

One of his men, going ashore for wood, was speared by natives. Later that day, the sailors retaliated, firing on three natives in a canoe and killing one of them. Flinders was greatly displeased, but it was a very difficult situation, and the extreme weather conditions were telling on his men. On the same day, another of his marines died in a frenzy, from sunstroke. The *Investigator* itself was in a desperate condition, quite incapable of withstanding a storm, and after brief explorations in Arnhem Bay and the Wessel Islands, Flinders judged that it was time to be gone. He recorded: 'In addition to the rotteness of the ship, the state of my own health and that of the ship's company were urgent to terminate the examination here for nearly all had become debilitated from the heat and moisture of the climate.'

Apart from confirming what some had found before him and others were to find later, namely that the climate and the inhabitants of Arnhem Land were not easy for white men to handle, Flinders' most significant discovery was made on February 18, 1803. On that day, sailing amongst the English Company's Islands

(Flinders named these in honour of the East India Company — but the British one, not the Dutch one) he fell in with a fleet of praus from Macassar, in the Celebes. Flinders feared hostilities, but the Macassans were peaceable. Through the interpretation of a Malay crew member of the *Investigator,* Flinders learned from the Macassan chief, Pobassoo, that they had come to Arnhem Land to gather trepang, an edible sea-slug. Pobassoo revealed that his contingent of six praus, each of about twenty-five tons, was only part of a large fleet. Sixty praus, with about a thousand men, had left Macassar two months earlier to sail to Arnhem Land with the north-west monsoon.

Pobassoo told Flinders that the Macassan trepang fleets had been coming to Arnhem Land regularly for about twenty years. This was a gross underestimate, but Flinders wasn't

left: Mimi figures in hunting scene, Obiri Rock

below: Spirit Figures and Barramundi X-Ray style, Nourlangie

to know it. He was impressed by the chief and he named an island for him, Pobassoo Island. The strait where he had encountered the Macassan fleet was put down on Flinders' charts as Malay Road.

In 1817, Philip Parker King, the son of the former Governor of New South Wales, was sent from Port Jackson in the *Mermaid* to complete the charting of the Australian coast. King sailed through Bass Strait and the Great Australian Bight, up the coast of Western Australia, and arrived at Arnhem Land in March, 1818.

King found the Macassan trepang fleets were back in greater numbers than ever. Fearing hostilities, he raised the British flag, and the Macassans' praus replied by showing the Dutch colours. The Dutch, with their strong grip on the East Indies, were the only

right: **Arnhem Land's only painting of the Fly River Turtle, common in Papua New Guinea**

below: **Art gallery in rock shelter, Arnhem Land**

91

white men that Macassans normally encountered. In fact, the Macassan word for a white man was 'ballander' a derivation of 'Hollander'. Through their contacts with the Macassans, the Arnhem Land Aborigines adopted this word, and 'ballander' is still the term they use for a white man.

But Captain King knew nothing of the complex Dutch/Malay influences in Arnhem Land culture. His only contact with the natives was in fending off an armed attack by them, while he and his party were examining a mangrove inlet. He was rather more successful with the Macassans, and he named Malay Bay in memory of their peaceful encounter.

King discovered and named many of the important features of the Arnhem Land vicinity on this and subsequent journeys. Ironically, he bypassed as unpromising the only bay which would eventually support a large and permanent white settlement on the north coast of Australia. King noted, after rounding Melville and Bathurst Islands: 'To the south was a deep opening, trending to the south-east of a river-like appearance; but, as it did not seem to be of sufficient importance to detain us, we passed on to the westward.' It was not until 1839, and the third Australian voyage of the *Beagle*, that Captain Wickham and Lieutenant Stokes examined that 'deep opening' and named it Port Darwin, for the famous naturalist. (Later, as Darwin, it became the only Australian State or territorial capital named after a scientist; most were named after British politicians.)

King, however, felt that he had discovered some places with interesting possibilities for settlement. Cape Croker, the northernmost point of the Northern Territory, and Croker Island, were named by him for the First Secretary of the Admiralty. Sheltering below Croker Island, on the northern tip of the peninsula which he named Cobourg Peninsula, 'after His Royal Highness Prince Leopold', King found a place which he considered a good anchorage, and he called it Raffles Bay.

A few days later, he discovered another harbour which impressed him even more and which he named for Vice-Admiral Sir William Essington. King wrote: 'As a harbour, Port Essington is equal, if not superior, to any I ever

saw, and from its proximity to the Moluccas and New Guinea, and its being in the direct line of communication between Port Jackson and India, as well as from its commanding situation with respect to the passage through Torres Strait, it must, at no very distant period, become a place of great trade, and of very considerable importance.'

A fortnight later, King discovered three large rivers, fringed with mangroves and with large saurians basking on the mud. He named them the Alligator Rivers, and they are still known as the East, South and West Alligator. But it was a mistaken observation. There are no alligators in the Northern Territory, only crocodiles.

King's observations about the prospects of settlement were even further from the mark and had more tragic consequences. In theory they might have been true, assuming that the theory was formulated by gazing from a considerable distance at a globe, but they ignored the practical difficulties which King and every white sailor before him had encountered in the North — the extremes of the weather, the hostility of the native population and the sheer remoteness from supplies and facilities of any kind that a white population would expect.

The next forty years saw a number of abortive attempts to establish places 'of great trade, and of very considerable importance' on the north coast of Arnhem Land. The first outpost was begun at Fort Dundas, Melville Island, in 1824. It was abandoned four years later after the fort's surgeon and another officer had been speared to death in clashes with wild Tiewi tribesmen.

In 1827, Captain James Stirling with HMS *Success* and three transports tried to establish a settlement at Raffles Bay, but it was abandoned in 1829. Raffles Bay failed even more quickly than Fort Dundas but for the same reasons — climatic extremes, tropical diseases and the unrelenting hostility of the blacks.

Further attempts to found white settlements at Port Essington and Escape Cliffs also failed. The Port Essington project lasted longest and was the only one that ever looked like succeeding. It was begun in 1838, and when Wickham and Stokes arrived the following year in the *Beagle* they found that the building of the settlement (which was called Victoria) was well under way. Returning a month later, they found a delighted crowd in attendance at the first white theatrical performance in Arnhem Land. The play was performed in a workshop, and tickets were issued with the legend 'Victoria Theatre, Port Essington, August 24th, 1839'.

The settlement was still there six years later when the first white expedition arrived by land from the south. Ludwig Leichhardt, after a desperate journey in which his colleagues Roper and Calvert were wounded and Gilbert was killed by Aborigines, arrived at the valley of the South Alligator River. Fighting their way through the dense forests of pandanus and tea-tree and negotiating the edges of the tidal swamps, Leichhardt's party reached the Cobourg Peninsula, and on December 17, 1845, Leichhardt recorded:

'We came on a cart road which wound round the foot of a high hill; and having passed the garden, with its fine cocoa-nut palms, the white houses, and a row of snug thatched cottages burst suddenly upon us; the house of the Commandant being to the right and separate from the rest. We were most kindly received by Captain Macarthur, the Commandant of Port Essington, and by the other officers, who, with the greatest kindness and attention, supplied us with everything we wanted.'

Leichhardt was the first white explorer to traverse the interior of Arnhem Land and it is probable that he became, three years later, the first white man to die there. The fate of Leichhardt's 1848 expedition remains the greatest mystery in Australian exploration, but it is known that he intended to strike northwards towards the Gulf of Carpentaria and then west in a bid to cross the entire continent to the shores of the Indian Ocean.

A tree on the Gregory River, marked with Leichhardt's symbol, indicates that he was heading north-west towards the Roper River, which he had named in 1845, and which forms the southern border of Arnhem Land. At Elsey Creek, an upper tributary of the Roper (and later famous as the setting of Mrs Aeneas Gunn's story *We of the Never Never*), A. C. Gregory in 1856 found what he believed were the traces of Leichhardt's last camp. Gregory wrote in his journal:

'Several trees cut with iron axes were noticed near the camp. There was also the remains of a hut and the ashes of a large fire, indicating that there had been a party encamped there for several weeks; several trees from six to eight inches diameter had been cut down with iron axes in fair condition, and the hut built by cutting notches in standing trees and resting a large pole therein for a ridge; this hut had been burnt apparently by the subsequent bush fires, and only some pieces of the thickest timber remained unconsumed.

'Search was made for marked trees, but none found, nor were there any fragments of iron, leather or other material of the equipment of an exploring party, or any bones of animals other than those common to Australia. Had an exploring party been destroyed here, there would most likely have been some indications, and it may therefore be inferred that the party had proceeded on its journey.

'It could not have been a camp of Leichhardt's in 1845, as it is 100 miles southwest of his route to Port Essington, and it was only six or seven years old, judging by the growth of the trees; having subsequently seen some of Leichhardt's camps on the Burdekin, Mackenzie and Barcoo Rivers, a great similarity was observed in regard to the mode of building the hut, and its relative position in regard to the fire and water supply; and the position in regard to the great features of the country was exactly where a party going westward would first receive a check from the waterless tableland between the Roper and Victoria Rivers, and would probably camp and reconnoitre ahead before attempting to cross to the north-west coast.'

Wherever Leichhardt went, it wasn't to the white settlement at Port Essington. If, by some chance, he was still wandering in the bush a year later, and came to Port Essington, he'd have found no white settlement. It was abandoned in 1849; another of the long string of settlement failures. Up to this point, the white man's experience in the north had been most discouraging and few would have disagreed with the earliest Dutch verdict on the place. It seemed that there was 'no good to be done there'.

In 1869, the white man tried again. The South Australian Government sent the Surveyor-General, George W. Goyder, to Port Darwin with a party of 135 men and instructions to lay out a new town. This town, Palmerston, would probably have failed like all the others except for one circumstance. It became the northern terminus for the Overland Telegraph Line, built across the centre of Australia from Adelaide in 1872.

From that time, Palmerston had a genuine reason for existence, as the landfall for Australia's cable link to Europe. Nevertheless, it was a struggling place for half a century. It was not until 1911 that it officially became Darwin, capital of the Northern Territory.

Even in the years since then, Darwin has not had it easy, and as late as the 1970 s, when it was devastated by a cyclone, the question was raised whether North Australia was a practical place to site cities. But with the regrowth of Darwin, the gradual spread of pastoral settlement, and the new populations attracted by mining ventures, much of the Northern Territory could now be classed as permanently settled by white men.

Arnhem Land was, and remains, a different story. Once the name meant the whole top end of the Northern Territory, between the Roper River and the Victoria River. Now Arnhem Land means a roughly square block of land, slightly bigger than Tasmania, and lying to the east of Darwin. It is bordered by the East Alligator River, the Arafura Sea, the Gulf of Carpentaria, and the Roper River, and since 1931 it has been an Aboriginal Reserve.

Arnhem Land today is the home of seven and a half thousand full-blood tribal

below: **Preparing an earth oven to cook flying foxes**

Aborigines. Until recently, few white men had ever lived there. Few, except for missionaries, Aboriginal Affairs officers, crocodile shooters and the odd adventurous pastoralist, saw any reason to live there. A couple of things have happened to change that now, but for most of its history — that is, its history as seen by white men — Arnhem Land has been generally regarded as just about the last place on earth.

The black version of Arnhem Land history is the exact opposite. For the Aborigines, Arnhem Land is the first place on earth, the birthplace of their spirit and their nation. Admittedly, there is no single black version of history, any more than there is a single white version. Every tribe in Australia has its own explanation of how the world began and how it operates. Even within Arnhem Land sixty different languages and dialects are still spoken, and it is no easy matter to trace the common beliefs that lie beneath the varied legends of sacred places and mighty events and totem heroes.

right: **Rock shelter, Arnhem Land Escarpment**

below: **Weathered rocks on Arnhem Land**

But Arnhem Land, the richest and longest-occupied of all Aboriginal lands, is the stronghold of Aboriginal culture, and the place where the Aborigines developed their art, ritual and legend to the highest degree. The reason was not cultural isolation. Even before the arrival of the white man, Arnhem Land was the most visited of the Australian coasts and the tribes who lived there were possibly the only Australian Aborigines who recognised the existence of a world outside this continent. But like other strong cultures, such as the Balinese, they absorbed these outside influences and built them into their own culture.

Consider the Yirrkala version of history. They believe that life began for them at Jelangbara, a place on the northern tip of Port Bradshaw in the extreme north-east corner of Arnhem Land. Here, they say, a group of spirit ancestors, the Djangawu, arrived by boat from an island to the north, landed on the beach, and set forth to create the landscape and the people. The Djangawu, who are the subjects of a major Arnhem Land song cycle, were a brother, two sisters, and a mysterious male companion. They carried with them certain magic objects. The Djangawu brother carried long painted and feathered poles, which were fertility symbols. At one place where he plunged the pole into the ground, a spring gushed forth. Other poles, planted in the ground, sprang into living trees, The Djangawu sisters, as they travelled across the country, gave birth to many living beings, who were the ancestors of the present tribes.

According to tribal legend, the magic objects were at first in the keeping of the Djangawu sisters, but one day, the Djangawu brother and his male companion stole the ritual objects, and ever since then the male members of the tribe have been the guardians of the sacred objects, songs, dances and rituals, and bear the responsibility of keeping them safe and handing them down to new generations.

Every detail and incident of the Djangawu story is preserved in the present-day ritual dances of East Arnhem Land. As Wandjuk Marika, an elder of the Reiritjingu clan, tells the story, the Djangawu travelled from Jelangbara right across to Millingimbi and Western Arnhem Land, creating all the people,

animals, birds, trees and places as they went. In each place where they sat down, they created a different tribe with a different language.

That is the eastern legend. The Western Arnhem Land tribes have their own creation myths and Dreamtime heroes. There are the Wawaluk Sisters, the Lightning Brothers, and the Waramurugundji, who flew down the western side of Arnhem Land and created the mighty rock escarpment. There is the Rainbow Serpent, who appears under various names, but is always regarded as a spirit of awesome power, and there is Jambuwul, the Thunder Man, who travels about on the cumulus clouds and sheds the life-giving rain on the earth below. This rain is life-giving in more than the ordinary sense. The raindrops contain tiny spirit children, who travel to the earth seeking a human mother.

In Arnhem Land, this Aboriginal lore is recorded in many ways other than through the human transmission of stories, songs and dances. In the east, the mythology is expressed in symbolic paintings on weapons, artefacts, and sheets of bark, but unfortunately these materials are perishable, or easily taken away. However, in the west, there are permanent records of the Aboriginal occupation, and the Aboriginal version of Arnhem Land. They are painted in red and yellow ochre, white pipe-clay and black charcoal, in the cave galleries of the Arnhem Land escarpment. There are friezes of up to a hundred feet long, sometimes with the later paintings super-imposed over the earlier. Several quite distinct styles are evident. There are Mimi paintings, which depict stick-like fast-running creatures. The Aborigines say that these are pictures of an earlier spirit people, and that they were painted by those people, not by the ancestors of the present Arnhem Land tribes. There are X-ray paintings, illustrating the internal bones and organs of human beings, animals, birds and fish. There are sorcery paintings in which the artist depicts the fate that he had in mind for his intended victim, and there are naturalistic paintings, dating from ancient to quite recent times.

Taken together, these cave galleries of Arnhem Land constitute the Louvre of early man, and they are arguably as important as the modern Louvre. They date back to an era of which we are massively ignorant; an era 150 centuries before the building of the Pyramids, 170 centuries before the fall of Troy, 180 centuries before the birth of Christ. Their importance can be stated in several ways. They represent the world's most massive and coherent depiction of the mind of man at a time when all men were nomadic huntsmen and fishermen, and they represent the passing of the long centuries as such men saw them.

The earliest edge-ground stone axes discovered in Arnhem Land have been estimated to be more than 20 000 years old, and the earliest ochre paintings are reckoned to be nearly that age. There are paintings depicting tribesmen hunting plains animals, such as kangaroos, with boomerangs. Arnhem Land ceased to be open grassy plains over 10 000 years ago when the sea-level rose, the climate changed, and the country became densely forested, and quite an impractical place to use boomerangs. There are paintings of the Thylacine, or Tasmanian Tiger, extinct in the north for at least 8 000 years.

Leaving aside for a moment the insights that we can gain into the mind of a primitive tribal society from the ancient oral and painted lore of the Aborigines, it is worth noting that they convey historical information which is valuable from anyone's point of view. They state, in one form or another, that the ancestors of the Aborigines came a very long time ago from the seas to the north; that different waves of people came to Arnhem Land in ancient times; that the climate changed, and that the flora and fauna changed, and the life of the people with it. All that may be common knowledge now, but it was not exactly on every white man's lips in the days of Captain Flinders, whereas the Aborigines had known it for centuries.

They also knew more than Flinders did about The Macassans. Pobassoo, the chief that Flinders met at Malay Bay, told him that the trepang fleets had been coming to Arnhem Land for twenty years. In fact, they had been coming to that territory, which they called Marege, for some two hundred years. The Aborigines recorded in their cave paintings the Macassan comings and goings, their praus,

their camps, and their smoke-houses, where they dried out the trepang. Some Aborigines went back to Macassar with the trepang fleets, and some stayed there to mix their blood into the Macassan strain. But others returned to tell the tale — there is an Arnhem Land cave painting of a monkey in a Macassan tree, as remembered by an Aborigine. Arnhem Landers also gained a strain of Macassan blood from the sexual relations between the visiting trepangers and the native women, although it seems, from the many song cycles that concern the Macassan people, that women were one of the two causes of friction in the usually harmonious relationships between these peoples. The Macassans didn't always ask before they took.

The other cause of friction was alcohol, which the Macassans introduced to Arnhem Land as an item of trade in return for trepang and pearlshell, and which the Aborigines, with their hunters' tradition of eating and drinking their fill of whatever they captured, handled very badly. The Macassans also introduced tobacco, 'batariva', and left behind them other traces — the tamarind trees which they planted around their camps, the notion of the dugout canoe, and the words 'lipa-lipa' for canoe, 'birita' for rice, and, as mentioned earlier 'ballander' for white man.

Although the Arnhem Landers aped certain of the Macassan habits — they took to smoking the long Macassan pipes, and many affected the pointed Macassan beard — their culture was not greatly affected, and their confidence in their future was undisturbed. They knew the Macassans were mere seasonal visitors, with no designs on their territory. But when the 'ballander' or white man, arrived, it was another story. The Aborigines painted him as they saw him — a gunboat bristling with cannons; a man firing a pistol; a man, with his hands in his pockets, issuing orders. They sensed that the white man had designs on their country. They replied with violence, and the white men did the same. The whole cycle of bloodshed and revenge, of stealthy black raids and punitive white expeditions, never really ceased until Arnhem Land was declared an Aboriginal Reserve in 1931.

above: **The old fishing hole**

opposite: **'The bones of nature laid bare'**

Even in this strongest and most traditional of the Aboriginal homelands, the lives of the natives had by then reached the crossroads. Some preferred to abandon tribal ways and gravitate to white men's cities. Those who remained have tried to preserve traditional ways, and in the last few years have even attempted to reverse history and leave the government and mission settlements to re-adopt a fully tribal life, existing on hunted bush tucker in their own original clan territories.

Unfortunately for these people, the white man has at last discovered something that he wants in Arnhem Land. A big bauxite-mining town already operates at Gove, not far from where the Djangawu landed in the Dreamtime. Vast uranium deposits have been discovered in the Western Arnhem Land escarpment, the repository of so much of mankind's early history. There is a danger that Arnhem Land, which these Aborigines see as the birthplace of their history, could become the crematorium of their history.

We should be clear about what we are doing. To destroy the sacred places of Arnhem Land is to destroy the meaning of life for its original people. It is the equivalent of demanding of all Israelis that they abandon not only their land, but their religion. The future is never going to be easy for the Australian Aborigine, even in the few places where he can cling with any security to his ancient beliefs. He has a right to his vision of the world; it worked well enough for him in the past. And we have no right to make his way harder, or to destroy a history which is not only his, but also ours and the world's. It is the story of humanity.

THE FLINDERS RANGES

In October, 1789, a fifteen year old Lincolnshire lad named Matthew Flinders joined the Royal Navy. His uncle, John Flinders, who had spent eleven years in the navy without making any visible impression, tried to dissuade him and so did other well-meaning friends. But Matthew said he was 'induced to go to sea against the wishes of my friends from reading *Robinson Crusoe.*' Perhaps it would have been better for Matthew Flinders had he heeded the advice of his friends, stayed at home and read *Robinson Crusoe* more closely, because his later career was not unlike that of Defoe's shipwrecked hero.

Flinders sailed to Port Jackson with Governor Hunter in 1795 as a midshipman in the *Reliance*. A year later he and another Lincolnshire man, George Bass, were almost drowned while exploring the coast south of Sydney in the *Tom Thumb*. In 1803, as a passenger on the *Porpoise*, he was wrecked on a sandbank 740 miles from Sydney and he sailed one of the ship's boats back to Sydney to organise the rescue of the other ninety-three survivors. At the end of the same year, while sailing back to England as the commander of the *Cumberland*, Flinders found the schooner leaking so badly that he was forced to put in at the French possession of Mauritius, not knowing that war had again broken out between France and England. He was taken prisoner and was not released for six and a half years from his island prison.

When finally he arrived back in England in 1810, it was to the greeting of a wife with whom he'd shared only three months of married life before being parted for nine years. During that same 1801 stay in England in which he had married Ann Chappell (and been refused permission by the Admiralty to have her accompany him back to Australia), he had published his first book *Observations on the Coasts of Van Diemen's Land, on Bass's Strait, etc.* Now he laboured unremittingly to complete the charts of his voyages and to write his great work *A Voyage to Terra Australis*. But Flinders was worn out by the extraordinary misfortunes of his life. When he was thirty-nine, his wife told a friend that he looked like a man of seventy. When he was forty, he died. The first copy of *A Voyage to Terra Australis* came off the press the day before he died and his wife placed it beside his bed, but Flinders was already unconscious and he never saw his major book.

It might have been the better for Flinders had he never gone to sea, but it would certainly have been the worse for Australia. With Bass, in the *Norfolk*, he had discovered Bass Strait, a most significant discovery in early Australian history since it considerably reduced the length of a ship's voyage from England. As captain of the *Investigator*, Flinders became the first man to circumnavigate the Australian continent and to chart great portions of the coast. He was an outstanding cartographer and an important discoverer — his sea explorations added up to the greatest single contribution to man's knowledge of the Australian coast. He was also a fine sea-captain, despite the fact that he was regularly sent to sea in leaky old tubs.

Flinders was the first man to use consistently the name that was eventually adopted for this continent — Australia — and he also bestowed a multitude of names on the features of the Australian coastline, beginning with the First Lord of the Admiralty, Earl Spencer, continuing through the names of various high officials and benefactors in England and the names of his associates and crew members in Australia, and ending with place names from his native Lincolnshire.

No white explorer gave more names to Australian places than Flinders. There was one later explorer, Major Mitchell, who tried to outdo Flinders in this regard, and who did not scruple to bestow his own names on features which he knew had already been named by earlier explorers. But some of Mitchell's names failed to stick.

Flinders was never so besotted with British royalty as the explorers of the middle nineteenth century who appeared to think that everything in Australia from a wombat hole to a giant desert had to be named for either Victoria or Albert, but one could wish that he had named fewer places after his patrons in the Admiralty and more from his own observations and experiences (as, for instance, he named Malay Road, off the west of Arnhem Land, because of his encounter there with the Macassan trepang fleet).

However, although Flinders immortalised many lesser men by bestowing their names on Australian geographical features, it must be noted that he never named a single spot for himself. Everything in Australia that bears his name — Flinders Bay, Flinders Chase, Flinders Island, the Flinders Group, the Flinders River and the Flinders Ranges — was named in his memory by later men. Of all of them the Flinders Ranges are the most fitting memorial to the great navigator. Just as Matthew Flinders staggers the mind by his achievements, these mountain ranges, the biggest in South Australia, stagger the eye with their rugged grandeur. And they contain many of the secrets of Australia, secrets that Flinders sought to discover as he sailed around the continent. He sighted them in 1802 when he sailed to the head of the gulf that he named Spencer Gulf for the First Lord of the Admiralty. His main interest was to discover if this gulf was the mouth of a strait which divided Australia into an eastern and western island.

He found that it was not (although we now know that it was once, one hundred million years before the *Investigator* sailed the waters of Spencer Gulf). As Flinders came to the shallows at the head of the Gulf, he noted:

'At noon, the furthest hummock seen from the anchorage was distant four or five miles; it stands on a projection of low sandy land, and beyond it was another similar projection to which I gave the name Point Lowly. This was the furthest visible part of the western shore; but the eastern land there approached within seven or eight miles, and extended northward, past it, in a chain of rugged mountains, at the furthest end of which was a remarkable peak.'

From the *Investigator's* anchorage, Flinders' artist, William Westall, made the first sketch of this 'chain of rugged mountains'. The next day, Westall set off in a party led by Lieutenant Brown to climb the highest peak that they could see in the north of the ranges. They estimated that its distance from the shore was five miles. In fact it was fifteen miles and the landing party had a strenuous hike before them, followed by a climb of over 3 000 feet.

But with commendable resolution, they climbed the mountain (later named Mount Brown) and spent a very uncomfortable night camped on its slopes.

It was a deceptive country. Not only was the mountain three times further away than they'd thought, but it was at the southern end, not the northern end, of that 'chain of rugged mountains' that they'd sighted from the ship.

The *Investigator* sailed away, and it was another thirty-seven years before the next white men ventured into those mountains. In 1839, the year that Governor Gawler named them the Flinders Ranges in honour of the noble Matthew, the explorer Edward John Eyre came through the mountains, seeking a path into the centre of Australia. He was foiled by the great saltpan of Lake Torrens, and he distributed a few names around the country to express his feelings — names like Mount Disappointment and Mount Hopeless.

The pastoralists, who were expanding their holdings north from the initial settlement at Adelaide, thought better of the country than Eyre did, and they occupied the southern ranges of the Flinders in the 1840 s. By 1850 they had reached the central point of the Ranges, Wilpena Pound, and by 1860 they had penetrated to the northern fastnesses of the Flinders. By then it was known that the Ranges extended for hundreds of miles in a great horseshoe that rose at Crystal Brook in the south and curved up past the head of Spencer Gulf to the north and east, finally plunging back into the flat plains near Lake Calabonna, not far below Lake Eyre, the vast saltpan in the 'dead heart' of Australia.

Wilpena Pound, the central feature of the Flinders Ranges, was discovered, along with the Arkaba Creek and Aroona Creek, by a teamster called William Chace in 1850. Chace was a controversial figure, unpopular with the wealthy interests in South Australia because he had tried to organise a teamsters' strike at the not long opened copper mines at Burra Burra. The gentry sneered at him as 'Chace the dray-lawyer' and 'the notorious bullock-puncher from the Burra Burra'. Although Chace Range is named after him, he was given little or no credit for his discoveries at the time. However, the pastoralists didn't hesitate to

follow his tracks into this new country and by 1851 they had established themselves in the Central Flinders. Wilpena Station was founded by Henry Strong Price in that year and pioneer squatters such as the Browne brothers, the Marchants, and Frederick Hayward soon established other interests in the area.

It was the Marchant brothers who gave the name of St Mary's Peak to the highest mountain at Wilpena Pound. The legend is that they saw it covered by a white mantle of snow and felt that it conveyed an overwhelming impression of saintliness. In later years, local settlers made derisive jokes about this legend. The Central Flinders area was so dry, in their experience, that they thought the Marchants could only have seen snow after a prolonged bout with colonial rum. Now it seems that the legend was not so laughable because St Mary's Peak has been capped by snow several times in the past few years. It is no

left: **Hills of Arkaba — 'arrested waves forever on the point of breaking'**

below: **Mysterious ancient carvings, Sacred Canyon**

longer the mysterious mountain that the first settlers sighted. Nowadays it's a popular target for the more energetic hikers from the nearby Wilpena Chalet. It's still a stiff climb, but there is a made path to the top and the climber is rewarded by views of some of the most glorious scenery that Australia can offer.

Wilpena Pound is a huge natural amphitheatre within a ring of mountains of which St Mary's Peak is the tallest. The Pound was created by the buckling of the earth's crust millions of years ago, and it is a place of many legends. The Aborigines called it Wilpena, meaning 'place of bent fingers', and from certain angles the mountains may be seen to resemble the side view of a hand held upwards with the fingers clenched. The artist Hans Heysen described more vividly the way the mountains appear to flow along behind one another in a saw-toothed pattern. He called them 'arrested waves, on the verge of breaking'.

right: **George Hunt and red gums at Wilpena station**

below: **Ripples of ancient ocean at Barraranna Gorge**

One of the mountains ringing the Pound is called Mount Sawtooth. Others bear Aboriginal names — Mount Boorong, Wangara Hill, Binya Peak, Mount Karawarra — and there's another category altogether, a series of hills and mountains which sound as if they were named by a practical joker. There's Madge Hill, Reggie Nob, Beatrice Hill, Dorothy Peak, Dick Nob, Walter Hill, Fred Nob. They are the work of a surveyor who couldn't think of any other names and named these features for his family, relatives and in-laws. One particular title he bestowed, Snave Hill, caused a good deal of puzzlement, until it was realised that the surveyor had found yet another way to perpetuate his family. The curious and somewhat repulsive word 'Snave' was no more than the surveyor's family name, Evans, spelt backwards.

Many of the major peaks of the Flinders Ranges, such as Mount Painter and Freeling Heights, were named for early surveyors, but one of the most interesting features at Wilpena Pound was named for a man who only *claimed* to be a surveyor. It is Rawnsley's Bluff, at the southern end of the Pound, and it commemorates one H. C. Rawnsley, who arrived in South Australia in 1850 and announced that the British Government had appointed him the Assistant Engineer of the colony.

This was news indeed to the South Australian Government which had not been notified of the appointment and had never heard of Rawnsley. However, the Governor apparently saw no reason to doubt Rawnsley's word. It sounds now like an incredibly gullible action, but there were a lot of pressures at work in South Australia at that time and one was an urgent call for government surveyors to get out to the frontiers, where the pastoralists were expanding, and start taking measurements and making maps.

By the end of 1850 a number of pastoralists had ridden as far as the Central Flinders, and had submitted to the Government their plans for their proposed runs. But the picture was totally confused because there were no agreed boundaries or points of reference, and the plans overlapped and contradicted each other most amazingly. Therefore, the Government hastily despatched a survey party to the Flinders. At its head was the newly arrived H. C. Rawnsley.

The Government soon found that the party it had despatched in such urgency was not carrying this urgency through into its daily operations. In fact, it was moving at such a sluggish pace, and covering so little ground, that the Government sought information about what it was doing and what was the trouble. Reports came back that the trouble was Mr Rawnsley, who did not appear to know what he was doing. The Government was informed that the survey of the Flinders Ranges, if it continued to be conducted according to Mr Rawnsley's methods, was unlikely to be completed before the end of the century.

But Rawnsley did not last that long. Once suspicions were aroused, enquiries to London revealed that the British Government had *not* appointed him as Assistant Engineer of the colony. In fact, like the South Australian Government, they had never heard of H. C. Rawnsley. Within a year of his impressive beginning, Rawnsley was unmasked as an imposter and dismissed from the service of the Government. But his 1851 'survey' had not been a display of total lethargy; he had penetrated the Flinders as far as the region of Wilpena Pound and the settlers named the great wall at the southern end of the Pound, Rawnsley's Bluff. It was an apt name, since Rawnsley was not what he claimed to be, and I doubt if the irony was unintended. It remains today as the name of one of the most majestic features of Wilpena Pound but many tourists are unaware that it commemorates the name of an early colonial con-man.

Although Wilpena Pound nowadays is a tourist attraction, and a part of the Flinders Ranges National Park, attempts were made in earlier days to use it for grazing and farming. It was never, despite a local legend to the contrary, a holding pen for Captain Starlight's stolen cattle. That legend arose because the film Robbery Under Arms, with Peter Finch and David McCallum, was shot at Wilpena Pound in 1957. (The Wilpena Pound Chalet had to be doubled in size to accommodate the film cast and crew.) But August Helling, the man who later operated the first Birdsville mail coach, built a hut inside the Pound in 1880, and grazed a few head of stock there.

Later, his hut was taken over and enlarged by a family named Hill, who attempted to grow wheat in the Pound. It was an implausible venture, in a region hundreds of miles north of Goyder's Line of rainfall, and in a spot virtually inaccessible to any form of wheeled transport, but the Hills battled on till 1914 before they abandoned their outpost. The stone hut remains as the only building inside Wilpena Pound. It is in a bad state of repair and is covered inside from floor to roof by the graffiti of modern barbarians. But there are moves afoot to restore it as a memorial to a brave, if tragically mistaken, family.

The Wilpena Pound Chalet, which was opened in 1947 is situated outside the Pound and is the base for the modern tourist. Adelaide is only five hours' drive away, along a sealed road, and the Chalet at present attracts some 18 000 tourists a year. Another 40 000 a year stop at the adjacent caravan park.

The attraction of Wilpena Pound, apart from its magnificent mountain scenery, is the chance to explore a huge area which is still close to a state of nature. No stock are permitted inside the Pound now, and no vehicles can enter. The only access is by foot, through a narrow gap in the circling mountain wall, and a hiking track across the base of a huge tilted slab called Sliding Rock. Inside, the Pound has a thick cover of native pines, sugar gums, acacias and grass. It is still quite easy to get lost inside this huge basin and it is no place for the unwary or inexperienced hiker. Two people have died there within the last twenty years. One, a ten year old boy named Nicholas Bannon, perished tragically in 1959, when he became separated from two parties of hikers. Each party had thought that he was with the other. Despite a massive rescue operation involving the armed forces, helicopters, and hundreds of searchers, he could not be found. Years later, after a bushfire had cleared the vegetation, the bones of the boy were found, huddled in a gully halfway up the mountains.

Wilpena Station, which was established in 1851 on the Wilpena Creek, outside the Pound, is still going strong. The present owner, George Hunt, points proudly to homestead buildings that date back to the 1850s, when the station was 930 square miles, shore 70 000 sheep, and employed about fifty shepherds and station-hands on its various outstations. The hut where the explorer, John McDouall Stuart, camped overnight on his way to the north still exhibits its traditional pug-and-pine construction, with a thatched roof and a crazy herringbone-patterned floor, supposedly laid down by a runaway sailor.

A later, but equally famous visitor to Wilpena Station, was Hans Heysen in the 1920s. Heysen was fascinated by the great red gums in the Aroona Valley and the Brachina Gorge. He estimated their age at between nine hundred and three thousand years. Splitting the difference, you could say that they were there when Julius Caesar invaded Britain. Heysen was captivated, not only by the trees, but by the clear flat light, the sharply defined contours, and the rugged primitive character of the purple mountains around Wilpena Station, and he found in this area the subjects for some of his greatest paintings.

Further to the north and lying on the plains just west of the Flinders Ranges, Sir Thomas Elder's old station, Beltana, is still a going concern. It was to this station that Elder brought his first camels, and it was to this station that Ernest Giles came, in 1875, to pick up a team of camels for his assault on the Nullarbor Plain and the Great Victoria Desert.

However, the old town of Beltana, near the Station, is no longer a going concern; at least, not in the usual sense. This historic township grew up as a service centre for the surrounding stations and for miners who arrived when big copper deposits were discovered nearby in 1870. An Overland Telegraph Line Repeater Station was built at Beltana town in 1872. The railway line from Port Augusta arrived in 1881. (It went on to reach Marree in 1884, Oodnadatta in 1891 and eventually Alice Springs in 1929.) The combination of railways and mining brought considerable prosperity to Beltana, and it was for a time the headquarters of the Australian Inland Mission. However, it was a combination of the same factors, mining and railways, that eventually killed the town. The open-cut coal mining begun in the 1940s at Leigh Creek, 26 miles north of Beltana, drew population away from it and the construction of the standard gauge railway in 1956 from Port Augusta to Marree followed a route west of Beltana to achieve easier grades.

Beltana no longer had a reason for existence, and within ten years of the loss of the railway, the place was deserted and its old hotels and shops were falling down. Now, however, Beltana is undergoing a rebirth as something else, a Field Study Centre for students who come to study the history and geography of the old town and of the neighbouring Flinders Ranges. The rebirth of Beltana is entirely due to the commendable efforts of Ivan and Nancy Hull and their family. The Hulls have their headquarters in the old Railway Station and they have managed to buy many of Beltana's remaining buildings for the purpose of saving and restoring them.

Another old town, with a similar story to tell, is Blinman in the centre of the Ranges. It is the only town in Australia named after a shepherd with a wooden leg and it commemorates the discovery made by Robert 'Pegleg' Blinman in 1859. Blinman was a shepherd on Angorichina Station and he

left: **Stubbs waterhole, Arkaroola Creek**

below: **Ruins of homestead near Wilpena Pound**

habitually sat on the same rock while he watched his sheep graze. One day, he broke off a lump of the rock and it turned out to be rich copper ore. Henry and Thomas Martin, butchers of Adelaide, got wind of this find and secured mineral leases for the area, and mining began in the early 1860s. The Martins soon joined the ranks of the Adelaide rich. There is no record of 'Pegleg' Blinman doing likewise. But the mining town that was named for him enjoyed an early period of prosperity, and its population had increased to a total of one thousand people in the 1870 s.

The Blinman mine produced more than a million pounds worth of copper before it eventually closed in 1918. The spirit went out of Blinman when the mine died and there is not much to be seen there now — just a few cottages in a single street, a post office, and a graceful century-old pub which is fitfully patronised by the present population of twenty-five people.

right: **Tame emu at Arkaroola Village**

below: **Lake Frome, drunk dry by the serpent, Arkaroo**

As is often the case in Australia's abandoned mining towns, the most interesting place in Blinman is the cemetery. It contains a Royal Geographical Society monument to William Darton Kekwick, who accompanied John McDouall Stuart on his expeditions to place the British flag in the centre of Australia. It also contains the strangest and most lyrical epitaph that can be found in any Australian graveyard.

The Glass family were early settlers in this area; there is a place called Glass's Gorge a few miles north of Blinman. Ellen Glass died in 1855, before the town of Blinman even existed, and this epitaph, a curious compound of Shakespearean and Biblical tags, was presumably written by her husband:

> 'She being dead yet speaketh, sown in
> Weakness, raised in power, let him kiss
> Me with the kisses of the mouth for
> Thy love is better than mine, and I
> Will give her the morning star.'

Many minerals have been found in the Flinders Ranges. Some, like copper and silver-lead, have been mined in quantity. Others, like gold and precious stones — amethyst, emerald, ruby, garnet — have only been found in small pockets. The major mining operations of the moment, apart from the open-cut mining of brown coal at Leigh Creek, are a talc mine at Mount Fitton, near Lyndhurst, and a barytes mine near Oraparinna. But geologists are quite sure that the Ranges contain further valuable mineral deposits, particularly of that controversial mineral, uranium.

Uranium was first discovered near Mount Painter in the Northern Flinders Ranges in 1910, by W. B. Greenwood, the manager of Mount Serle Station. At that time the mineral was called radium and was in demand because of Madame Curie's experiments in the use of radium for treating cancer. The Greenwood family formed a company with an Adelaide University geologist, Douglas Mawson, to mine the radium and export it, but the project was defeated by the isolation of the site and the high cost of transporting the material by camel to Port Augusta.

In his later and more famous days, Sir Douglas Mawson returned to Mount Painter and amongst the geology students that he took on tour there in 1937 was a young man named Reg Sprigg. Seven years later, Reg Sprigg was back in the same area. He had been seconded from the army to work with scientists like Mark Oliphant on a joint American-British project which was so top secret that the scientists themselves weren't told what it was about. In time, they learned why they had been asked to restart the uranium mine at Mount Painter. The only information they'd gathered was that the uranium would be used to make atomic suns. When the truth emerged, they didn't know whether to be excited or frightened. It was all part of the Manhattan Project to create an atomic bomb, brighter than a thousand suns.

'Thin Man' and 'Fat Man', the bombs that fell on Hiroshima and Nagasaki, contained no uranium from the Flinders Ranges. But Australian uranium helped to develop the Manhattan Project, and a hole on the slopes of Mount Painter, which is still full enough of uranium to send geiger counters crazy, marks the entry of Australia into the atomic age. After the war, Exoil carried out further explorations in the Northern Flinders and blazed out a series of mountain roads and tracks for their vehicles. Today, these tracks serve a different purpose, as sightseeing roads for tourists from the Arkaroola Village.

Reg Sprigg had been interested in the Northern Flinders since his first geological expeditions in the 1930s, and in 1968, the Sprigg family purchased Arkaroola Station, the most mountainous sheep station in South Australia. They did not buy it for mining purposes, but with the intention of establishing a sanctuary and conservation area in what had become a rundown sheep station, infested by wild camels, donkeys, goats and feral cats. They also wished to operate the area as a controlled tourist resort, and today the Arkaroola Village is established as the tourist headquarters of the Northern Flinders. Native wild life, including the euro, or wallaroo, the red and the grey kangaroo, the yellow-footed rock wallaby and the brush-tailed wallaby, is once again thriving in the area.

Unfortunately, the wild goats are thriving just as mightily, and although about 5 000 of them are shot or otherwise got rid of every year, their numbers remain at about 15 000 at Arkaroola. Although the herds of mountain goats scurrying along the ridges add some superficial colour to the scenery, they are destructive to both the natural vegetation and the native wild life. They are a curse, bequeathed to the Flinders Ranges by a nineteenth century settler who had the brilliant idea of breeding an angora herd.

The chief attraction to tourists at Arkaroola is the fantastic mountain scenery which gives the impression of having been carved out of the living rock by some giant hand. The tribe that was once native to this region, the Andjanamutana people, believed that the mountains had been carved up, not by a giant hand, but by a giant snake. According to their legend, the giant serpent Arkaroo, which lived in the Dreamtime in Main Water Pound in the heart of the Gammon Ranges, was afflicted by thirst. He slithered down out of the plains and drank Lake Frome dry, turning it into the saltpan that it is today. Then Arkaroo dragged his bloated body back into the mountains. The sinuous gorge of Arkaroola Creek is the path that was carved by the serpent. The seven permanent waterholes along the Creek (Arkaroola Village is situated on one of them) are the seven relief stations where Arkaroo had to ease some of Lake Frome out of his bladder.

Finally, Arkaroo made his way back into the Gammon Ranges, and there he sleeps still. But it is an uneasy sleep. His belly still rumbles from all that salty water he drank at Lake Frome, and that is the reason for the earth tremors that shake the Flinders Ranges about once a week. They are the results of Arkaroo's big bellyache.

The geological explanation of the Flinders Ranges is not perhaps as poetic as the Aboriginal explanation, but it is just as fascinating. The tourists who rattle in four-wheel drive vehicles along the seventeen-mile ridgetop tour, winding along switchback trails and up implausible grades to finish on the very top of a mountain peak at Siller's Lookout, get more than hair-raising thrills and unbelievable mountain views. They get a chance to see how the world, and their own continent, was formed.

Reg Sprigg explains that the Arkaroola-Mount Painter region is one of extreme geological antiquity, with a core of granites nearly two billion years old. Australia was at that time a part of the southern supercontinent, Gondwanaland, which was centred around Antarctica. Pieces of Gondwanaland gradually broke away and drifted north. India drifted all the way to the continent of Asia, and the impact of the collision caused the thrusting up of the Himalayas, Africa, South America, and Madagascar also broke away from Gondwanaland. Australia eventually broke away too, being the last to go, and taking with it the marsupial animals. Australia is still drifting north at the rate of a few inches a year, and at some time in the future, if the world has not destroyed itself with the cosmic materials that may be mined from places like the Flinders Ranges, Australia will collide with Asia.

Until five hundred million years ago, the Flinders Ranges were the bed of a sea off the eastern coast of Australo-Gondwanaland, and were washed by the waters of Panthalassa, the ancestral Pacific Ocean. Figures like these are, of course, so immense that they are difficult to grasp in the abstract. The sensational thing about the Flinders Ranges is that there you can see those things in the concrete, embedded in the face of the rocks. The cup-shaped outline of Archaeocyatha, a sponge-coral-like animal, is clearly visible. This was the first animal to develop an obvious skeleton and was the springboard for the evolution of the higher forms of animal and plant life.

Even older are the ripples on the giant cliff-face at Barraranna Gorge. You can get some idea of the antiquity of this land, and the cataclysmic forces that created it, when you realise that this stupendous cliff, before it was thrust to the vertical by the buckling of the earth's crust, once lay flat. It was the bed of the sea, and the evidence is still there. The ripples on the cliff face were made by the waters of Panthalassa, more than a billion years ago.

Hans Heysen once described the Flinders Ranges as 'the bones of nature laid bare'. They are that, and more. They are the secrets of nature laid bare. The great navigator, Matthew Flinders, who himself unravelled so many of the secrets of Australia, has a fitting memorial in the Flinders Ranges, where the story of this continent from its earliest times is so spectacularly revealed.

opposite: **The Copper Kingdom**

below: **Sillers Lookout, at the end of the ridge top trail — Arkaroola**

LITTLE CORNWALL

South Australia in the nineteenth century earned a reputation as a 'paradise of dissent', because of the freedoms that it offered to people of every religious denomination. But, during the first few years of the colony, it might have been more aptly called a 'purgatory of dissent'.

The colony had been formed according to the abstract principles of Edward Gibbon Wakefield and it should, in theory, have proceeded smoothly from its foundation in December, 1836. The people who had already bought land orders worth £35 000 in London should have arrived to settle and work their land, and the sale of further land should have financed a regular flow of immigration to the colony.

What actually happened was that only a quarter of the people who had bought land orders came to settle in South Australia. The rest despatched their poor relations to look after their interests and many hoped to turn a quick profit by selling off their land at an increased price. But surveying and settlement of the land proceeded at a much slower pace than expected. There was too much speculation in land and too little work on it. The colony was existing on imported food supplies at ruinously high prices and the boatloads of immigrants contained too few men with capital and too many penniless labourers in search of non-existent jobs.

In 1841, the Board of Colonization Commissioners, which had been responsible for launching the new colony, went bankrupt and the situation in South Australia looked desperate. There was plenty of dissent, but most of it was the dissent of immigrants who believed they had been hoodwinked into coming to a place that offered no hope.

By good chance, the development that was to prove the salvation of South Australia occurred in the same year, 1841. Two Cornishmen, Thomas and Hutchins, found a vein of silver-lead ore in the foothills at Glen Osmond, just four miles from the centre of Adelaide. A company was formed to develop this find and the mine, the Wheal Gawler, commenced operations in May, 1841.

It was South Australia's, and all Australia's, first metal mine and a parcel of ore shipped to London from the Wheal Gawler was Australia's first mineral export. Although the Wheal Gawler's lode soon petered out and the mine failed to make a profit, it was South Australia's luckiest strike. That may sound paradoxical, but it was not the economic impact of the Wheal Gawler that counted. It was the dynamic effect that the discovery of this mine had on the climate of hope and confidence in the young colony.

The public suddenly became keenly interested in a little book called *The Mineral Kingdom of South Australia* which had been locally published in Adelaide in 1840. The author, a brilliant and unconventional German geologist named Johann Menge, had been employed in 1837 as a Mine and Quarry Agent by the South Australian Company and had spent a couple of years wandering about the country with a pick and a sample-bag.

Amongst many other perceptive observations, such as that the Barossa Valley would one day support a great wine industry, Menge predicted that South Australia would prove to be a rich mineral field. He reported finds of diamonds and other precious gems and ores bearing gold, silver, copper and iron.

When the finds of galena (silver-lead ore) at Glen Osmond proved that Menge had not been talking rubbish, prospectors of all kinds were quickly on the trail. Within the next ten years their discoveries earned South Australia a new title, 'the Mining Cradle of Australia'. It was a name that hard-headed colonists might have considered more comforting than 'Paradise of Dissent'.

The Wheal Gawler was also important in another way. It marked the first impact on South Australia of a people who were to do much to shape its fortunes — the Cornish people. 'Wheal' is the Cornish name for mine, and Gawler was the Governor of South Australia. Cornishmen discovered this mine, Cornishmen named it and Cornishmen worked it, as they worked the other silver-lead mines operating at Glen Osmond in the 1840s, the Wheal Watkins and the Gilles.

The lodes were rich but too small for profit and the mining operations at Glen Osmond ceased in 1851. The only traces to be seen now are some old underground tunnels, which are used by Woodley's to store their Queen Adelaide wines, and the stone chimney of the smelter, which was built in the round Cornish style and which still stands on the hillside overlooking the modern city of Adelaide.

By the time these mines closed, much more valuable mineral discoveries had been made in South Australia and the Cornish people were in great demand to work them. No race could boast a longer continuous experience in mining. The first tin deposits in Cornwall were worked as early as 2000 BC and Cornish tin was carried in trading ships to the far Mediterranean, centuries before the fall of Troy. But it was with the discovery of copper in Cornwall at the beginning of the eighteenth century that the Cornish began to develop the expertise in deep underground mining which they later exported to many corners of the world, including South Australia.

They brought with them to South Australia their technological inventions — the Cornish boilers and the high-pressure steam engines which powered the haulage cars in underground mines and saved the miner from the toil of fetching ore to the surface in a bag slung over his back. They also brought their individualistic notions of working organisation. Cornishmen did not like to work for wages. They preferred a piece-work system called 'tributing'. They would form themselves into groups and work together on a pitch, or portion of the lode, which was drawn by lot. They were paid an agreed percentage of whatever ore they mined, and they split the profits equally amongst their party.

Other colonists, who had imagined that a Cornishman was just an ordinary kind of Englishman, were surprised to find just how

below: **Miners' cottages, Burra**

different these people were. They had been, in ancient days, a separate kingdom with their own customs and their own language. Unlike the Welsh, they lost their separate language but many individual words from it were preserved, particularly in mining parlance, and became a part of Australian mining terminology — 'wheal' for mine, 'whim' for a mine haulage, 'winze' for an underground tunnel, 'platte' for a level surface leading off a shaft, 'crib' for a miner's lunch.

Although most of the language they spoke was English, it was English of a special kind, spoken in a thick brogue and employing all sorts of peculiar expressions and turns of speech. They commonly greeted each other as 'cousin', and because of this, the Cornishmen were soon known in South Australia as 'Cousin Jacks' and their wives as 'Cousin Jennies'. They called the mine manager 'Captain' or, rather 'Cap'n', and that also became an established practice in the South Australian Mines. They were a people of contradictions, and not just in their speech, although certainly they excelled in putting things in a way that made an Irishman sound comparatively straightforward. These are a couple of examples from Oswald Pryor, who was descended from a Cornish family at Moonta and who captured the essence of these people in his delightful cartoons: A workman, spanner in hand, indicates the new mine buildings and tells the bowler-hatted manager: 'Don't like to tell 'ee Cap'n, but they alterations is a bad improvement'; one old-timer, leaning on a stick and pointing out to another old-timer his particular cottage in a row of buildings, tells him: 'Mine's the one white-washed yeller'.

The Cornishmen were also contradictory in their life style. They were addicted to chapel and loved strong sermons, lusty hymns and attending revival meetings and funerals. However, they also liked rather less godly pastimes like cock-fighting, wrestling and drinking. They were fond of food and particularly insisted that the Cornish pasties cooked by their Cousin Jenny should come right up to the mark in both quality and quantity — a decent pasty for a miner's crib was one that he could rest on his knee by one end, while he attacked the other end.

They liked plenty of gloom and doom in their chapels, but were delightfully humorous in their pubs. They worked as little capitalists, but were often fiercely radical in their politics. And, although they called their bosses 'Cap'n' they were no great respectors of ranks and titles as such, and their respect had to be earned.

The Cornishmen all seemed to share the qualities of being hard workers and good miners and it was largely through their efforts that the mines of South Australia worked so well and pulled the colony out of a desperate situation and into an enviable one.

In 1842, Francis Dutton, a pioneer settler at Kapunda, forty-five miles north of Adelaide, was out after straying sheep one day when he noticed a bright green substance in an outcrop of rock. He broke off a piece of the rock and showed it to his neighbour, Captain Bagot. Bagot in turn showed Dutton a similar piece of rock, picked up in the same area by his son. Neither man was sure what the green material was, but both suspected that it was copper carbonate ore.

Dutton and Bagot acted quickly to secure ownership of this piece of land and they were lucky enough to be able to buy eighty acres around the rock outcrop for eighty pounds. Neither man had said anything about the mineral find until they could obtain the title-deed to the land, but they sent away a parcel of ore samples to London for assay. When the results came back, they learned that they were sitting on a fortune. The ore contained an average twenty-three per cent of copper. Some individual samples contained as high as seventy per cent of copper. Dutton and Bagot immediately formed a company to mine this bonanza.

Cornish miners were employed and they worked on a tribute of three shillings and sixpence for every pound's worth of ore mined. They did very well out of this particular deal because the rich ore, shipped from Port Adelaide to smelters at Swansea, in Wales, fetched very high prices: the average was nearly twenty-five pounds per ton. And the ore was there in quantity. Before it was closed in 1886, the Kapunda mine produced seventy thousand tons of copper, and over £1 000 000 in profit to its lucky owners.

Kapunda was the first big copper mine in Australia. And whereas the earlier silver-lead discoveries at Glen Osmond had revived the colony's flagging confidence in itself, the impact of Kapunda travelled much further and speculators in the other Australian colonies, and in Britain, suddenly became very interested in South Australia. Their interest grew to fever in 1845, when Australia experienced its first mining boom, and British speculators poured money into South Australian copper prospects with the same careless confidence that they exhibited in West Australian gold prospects half a century later. The cause of this excitement was another copper mine, which pushed even Kapunda into the shade. A hundred miles north of Adelaide, in country that was still sparsely settled grazing land, was a sheep-run called Burra Burra. The name, which is Hindustani for 'great great', was given to the sheep-run by Indian shepherds and it proved singularly prophetic. Burra Burra was to become the greatest copper mine in the world at the mid-nineteenth century.

A shepherd called Pickett discovered the Burra Burra lode and, indeed, for anyone who had any idea of what he was looking at, it must have been difficult to miss. The head of the lode stuck out of the ground like a great green bubble and it could be seen from quite a distance. Pickett passed on his information, for a price, to two Adelaide storekeepers, Alexander Thomson and James Bunce.

Burra Burra at this time was still Crown grazing land. According to the land laws of the time, such land could only be sold in lots of 20 000 acres at the price of one pound an acre. In other words, the purchase of the Burra Burra prospect required a sum of £20 000. Bunce and Thomson raced around Adelaide trying to form a syndicate which could raise this money. They ended up with a syndicate of eighty-six members, composed of various Adelaide interests including merchants, doctors, lawyers, and even blacksmiths and carpenters.

But, unknown to the Adelaide syndicate, another shepherd on Burra Burra had also sighted the green head of the lode and had passed on the information to local landed interests, including Dutton and Bagot of Kapunda. These formed a rival syndicate and the Governor of South Australia, Governor Grey, received simultaneous applications for the land from the two rival groups.

The stage was set for one of the most interesting battles in South Australian history — the battle between 'The Snobs' and 'The Nobs', as it became popularly known. The Nobs were the landowners and they were given that name because they were already men of substance and standing in the community. The motley collection who had formed the Adelaide Syndicate could not be described in the same way, but they certainly hoped to achieve greater wealth and standing by getting control of the Burra Burra copper prospect. They were would-be Nobs, and they were therefore dubbed the Snobs.

No love was lost between the two groups and neither of them wished to share the Burra Burra field with the other. Despite frantic efforts, the Snobs were unable to raise the full price of the land. But, since the laws of the day required that purchases of Crown land should be paid for in gold coin, the Snobs were able to foil the Nobs by withdrawing so many gold sovereigns from the banks that there was not enough gold left for the Nobs to make up the purchase price themselves.

Governor Grey, faced with a deadlock, resolved it according to the precepts of King Solomon. He had the Burra Burra survey divided into two equal portions, and the rival syndicates had to draw lots out of a canvas bag, and each pay £10 000. The Nobs won the southern half of the survey, and at first it seemed that they had enjoyed the luck of the draw. But the rich ore lying on the surface of the southern portion did not extend into an underground lode. Although the Nobs spent a good deal of money in trying to develop their mine, which they called the Princess Royal, they were unable to make any money. The land soon reverted to grazing and the only reminders that can be seen today of its claims to mining glory are a few holes in a hillside and a gracious and beautifully proportioned stone homestead named the Princess Royal.

The rich prize went to the Snobs. A vast lode of copper was found under the northern

portion of the survey. Even the surface ore was so rich that they were able to pick it straight up and ship it to the Swansea smelters. The returns were so good that they financed the further development of the mine. The Burra was probably the only big mine where shareholders were never called on to put in any more capital beyond their original subscriptions for the purchase. All further cash was raised, and development paid for, directly out of the profits of the mine.

The Burra became known as the 'Monster Mine'. It was also called 'The World's Wonder' and 'The Great Jeweller's Shop' and South Australia earned itself a new name, 'The Copper Kingdom', because of the operations at the Burra. The mine was so rich in copper that it was initially quarried rather than mined.

The 'Monster Mine' produced over five million pounds worth of copper: 364 426 tons of copper ore was the amount extracted over thirty years. (The same amount, in terms of the world copper prices of 1970, would have realised some $1 500 million). The mine was described as the salvation of South Australia and, it was reckoned, indirectly employed all of South Australia. Its economic impact went much further than the boundaries of the colony. For instance, one-third of the production of the coal mines at Newcastle in New South Wales was consumed by the Burra copper smelter. The mine workings directly employed nearly 1 200 men under Henry Ayers who was the first general manager of a large-scale mining operation in Australia. He was an outstanding success and later rose in Parliament with the support of the mining industry, was Premier of South Australia three times, was knighted and had Ayers Rock named after him.

Burra Burra itself was not so much a town as a collection of towns. Kooringa was the business centre, Aberdeen was the Scottish town, Lewisher the Welsh town, and Redruth the Cornish town. There were also German and Irish elements in the population of five thousand as well as native-born Australians from the eastern States. But, as usual in South

top: **Cornish dugouts, Burra Creek**

left: **Inside the dugout**

Australian mining towns, the Cornish were by far the biggest element. There were about fifteen hundred of them and not all of them chose to live in the company's cottages at Redruth. Poorer or thriftier Cornish families preferred to live rent-free in dugouts which they excavated in the banks of the Burra creek.

These dugouts can still be inspected and they are highly valued by the local people who are interested in preserving the remains of Cornish architecture and traditions. These incredible underground dwellings reveal what an appropriate name 'Burra' was for a settlement dominated by Cornishmen. It seemed to be in their blood to burrow like rabbits and they must have lived like rabbits in their creek-side caves; there was hardly enough room to do otherwise.

Most of these dwellings consisted of three or four tiny rooms connected by narrow tunnels. The roofs, made of logs, stone slabs and clay, were very low and even the Cornish, who were generally a short people, must have found it difficult to stand upright in the dugouts. The

top: **Cecil Ellis at miner's cottage, Moonta**

right: **Cooking Cornish Pasties, Moonta**

below: **Face of the Monster Mine, Burra**

walls and floors were mud, and the only exterior symbols to distinguish these dwellings from the caves of troglodytes were the chimneys that poked up through the roof or, rather, through the ground.

There were many hazards to life in the creekside and the cooking chimneys opened the way to one of them. Practical jokers were fond of dropping rocks, or more objectionable objects, down the chimneys into the cooking pots below. There was always the possibility of stray cows and horses falling through the roof, while flash floods sometimes roared down the Burra Burra Creek and washed away the furniture. The Cornishmen claimed that their dugouts were warm in winter and cool in summer but, with the lack of sanitation, their situation was not healthy and there were numerous cases of typhoid. The one undeniable advantage of the creek dwellings was that they were cheap.

Eventually, the main wave of the Cornish people moved on to new copper strikes further west of Burra Burra, but there are many reminders of them left in the town.

The last great copper strike of the nineteenth century in South Australia, and the last great Cornish rush to a new field, took place fifteen years after the opening of the Burra Burra mine. Again the agents of the discovery were shepherds although on this occasion they had some help from the native wild-life. And once again, as with the Nobs and the Snobs, there was a desperate race between two rival syndicates to secure the mining lease on the area.

Captain Walter Watson Hughes, a retired master mariner, had pastoral holdings at Walla-Waroo on the upper Yorke Peninsula, some hundred miles west of Burra Burra. The name of his property, in the language of the Naranga tribe, meant 'Wallaby urine', and around 1860 that could have been taken as a fair description of the property's pastoral prospects. Droughts and low wool prices were making life hard.

However, during a visit to Walla-Waroo from his head station at Watervale, Hughes noticed that the mallee root fires at his shepherds' camps gave off blue-green flames.

He knew this was a sign of copper and he instructed his shepherds to be on the lookout for copper ore. Not long afterwards a shepherd named James Boor discovered a mound of green carbonate of copper which had been thrown up out of its burrow by a marsupial rat. As soon as Hughes heard the news, he sent a team of four Cornish miners from Burra Burra to test the site. They selected the shaft in traditional Cornish fashion. One of them whirled a pick around his head, let it go, and they started to dig at the spot where it fell. It was a lucky throw; the shaft they dug ran straight down into the heart of a rich body of copper ore.

Hughes immediately pegged and registered a mineral lease and set up a private company to work the site which was soon known as Wallaroo. But soon afterwards, in 1861, another shepherd named Patrick Ryan came across a heap of green malachite pebbles at a place called Moonta, several miles from Wallaroo. Again, the original miner was a marsupial. This time, it was a wombat who'd thrown the material out of his hole. Ryan kept this to himself for some time but one day got drunk at Port Wakefield Hotel and spilled his secret to the proprietor, a Mr Johnston. Johnston immediately began to set up a syndicate to secure the mineral lease; however, Hughes got wind of the news and sped up to the Yorke Peninsula from Adelaide to interview Ryan. The shepherd, who was not a man of fearful intellect, had already shown the publican's syndicate the site and had agreed to receive a fifth share in the mine. Hughes, a swift operator, was able to persuade Ryan to show him the site and to sign a second agreement, giving him a tenth share in the mine and a retainer of six pounds per week.

Having obtained the necessary survey information, Hughes sent a young man named Horn galloping hell-bent to Adelaide to secure the lease. The publican's men were riding to Adelaide on the same mission and were seventeen hours ahead, but they did not know that a rival was on their tracks. Horn, with numerous changes of horses, rode nearly two hundred miles in eighteen hours and arrived in Adelaide at cock-crow the next morning to give the news to John Taylor, Hughes' agent in

Adelaide. The Mines Registrar's office opened at 10 a.m., and the publican's party arrived there on the dot. Taylor was a few minutes later. But the Chief Clerk arrived at ten minutes past ten. He did not know the other men but he knew Taylor and he called him to the counter first. Taylor applied for thirty sections at Moonta, each of eighty acres. When he'd left the office, the publican's men tried to register their claim, and were staggered to find that someone had got in before them.

Tremendous litigation followed over the next eight years, and Hughes' Moonta Company eventually agreed, out of Court, to pay the other syndicate £8 000 for their legal expenses. But Hughes had the mine, and the publican's syndicate had lost a fortune, through the chance arrival of a clerk at his office ten minutes late. Horn, the young man who had galloped that epic ride to Adelaide to turn the trick for Captain Hughes, had to eat all his meals standing up for the next week. Paddy Ryan, the discoverer of the Moonta Mine, drank himself to death on his six pounds a week retainer before the Moonta Mine paid its first dividend. But the Moonta-Wallaroo mines, once they came into operation, paid beyond everyone's dreams. They proved to be the last, the longest-lived and the richest of all South Australian mines.

Once again, the men who worked the mines and produced the wealth were Cornishmen. The owners, men like Captain Hughes, Sir Thomas Elder and Robert Barr-Smith, were not Cornishmen and neither were the other shareholders who received the rich dividends of the mine. There was some bitterness about this on a couple of occasions in the history of the mines, when the directors of the Moonta Mining Company forced the miners to take lower wages at the same time as they were declaring record dividends.

But, except for the Welshmen who specialised in smelter work, the miners, the engineers and the managers, or 'Captains', at Moonta, were Cornish almost to a man. And the most notable exception, Captain Henry Hancock, for many years the Superintendent of the mines, was considered an honorary Cornishman by the miners. Hancock had had the misfortune to be born five miles the wrong

side of the Tamar, in Devon, but he understood Cornish ways, and 'Cap'n 'Ancock' became one of the legendary figures in the history of the Moonta area.

Some of the Cornish miners came from Kapunda and Burra when they heard the news of this strike, but many more came direct from Cornwall itself. This immigration went on for years, and eventually the Cornish people were concentrated so heavily in the Moonta area that it became known as 'Little Cornwall'. They brought with them, as well as their mining expertise, their usual preoccupations, notably their obsession with religion. A century ago, there were twenty-five churches within the Moonta Town and Moonta Mines area. All but two of them were Methodist. Practically everyone went to church and went often — perhaps three or four times on one Sunday.

But the Cornish were such non-conformists in religion that they could not even conform to one brand of Methodism. Instead, there were three rival sects, the Wesleyans, the Bible Christians, and the Primitive Methodists, and they competed vigorously for souls. Not all of the churchgoing was from the most religious of motives. Jim Shields, who started work in the Moonta Mines when he was fourteen and worked there till they closed, recalls that in the latter days when jobs were getting scarcer the Captain might say to a Cousin Jack:

'Never seen you in Church, John, Sunday.'
'No. 'Aven't been there for weeks.'
'Well look, my son, I don't think you'd lose any ground if you'd come along two or three times of a Sunday to Chapel. That's all I've got to say to 'ee'.

There was, in other words, a certain climate of fear, not unusual in a company town. When one miner went to the office and complained: 'Well, if we can't get satisfaction, we'll go to the government', the Captain turned on him and said 'For your information, my man, we are the government'.

Life was never a picnic at Moonta. Typhoid epidemics, caused by bad drinking water, carried away hundreds in the early days and the rows upon rows of children's graves in the Moonta cemetery are the saddest monuments to the harshness of life and the frequency of

above: **Princess Royal Homestead, near Burra**

left: **Miner's cottage, Moonta**

opposite: **Hell's gates, entrance to Macquarie Harbour**

death in Little Cornwall. When the Moonta mines closed in 1923, many of the Cornish people went away. Although a few old-timers are left who call themselves 'Cousin Jacks' and speak with a faint brogue, the Cornish characteristics are fading out of the younger generations. One can still see a row of preserved miners' cottages at Moonta, and the great round Cornish Chimneys at the mine ruins, and the Methodist churches, now with much depleted congregations.

Attempts are being made now to revive Cornish festivals, but it isn't easy to recapture the genuine feeling. However, I hope that when tourists at Moonta eat their pasties, bulging with turnip, and drink their Swanky, a Cornish beer brewed in the bottle and judged ready to drink when the cork blows out of the bottle, they will eat and drink to the spirit of an indomitable people, who made their own peculiar and valuable contribution to Australia.

THE WILD WEST COAST OF TASMANIA

Anthony van Diemen, the son of a Dutch burgomaster, enlisted as a soldier in the service of the Dutch East India Company and arrived in Batavia in 1618. There he became a clerk and rose rapidly through the Company's ranks until eventually in 1636, he became Governor-General of the Dutch East Indies, a position he held until his death in 1645.

As Governor-General, he sent away from Batavia a sailor named Abel Tasman on several important voyages of discovery. On one of these voyages, in 1642, Tasman discovered the island now named for him, Tasmania. In his small war yacht, the *Heemskerk* and accompanied by the flute *Zeehan*, Tasman first sighted the west coast of Tasmania in the region of Macquarie Harbour. (A flute was a vessel of war carrying only part of her armament, to serve as a transport.) He sailed around the southern end of the island and at Forestier Peninsula he had his carpenter swim to the shore and plant the Dutch flag to take formal possession of the land. Tasman did not name this land after himself. He named it, after his Governor-General, 'Van Diemen's Land'.

By all accounts, van Diemen was an enlightened and progressive man. It is one of those ironies of history that the name of his land became an oath and an obscenity to the ears of the poorer classes of Britain from the day that it became a convict settlement in 1803 until the day that the name was officially changed to Tasmania in 1855. Even at this later date, the name was still used, and always in an unfavourable sense, to describe old lags who had migrated from Tasmania to the mainland. Many of the crimes and robberies committed on the Victorian goldfields in the 1850s were blamed, rightly or wrongly, on the 'Van Diemonians'. And from the beginning of the convict settlement, the street ballad-makers played on the fact that 'Diemen' sounded the same as the English word 'demon'. They struck terror into the hearts of their listeners with songs depicting Van Diemen's Land as a place ruled by demons, who treated convicts with monstrous cruelty.

There are so many versions of the transportation ballad called 'Van Diemen's Land' that modern folk-singers are at liberty to choose their own. But the song, in various guises, was widely known in England and Ireland by the year 1830. The names of the three poachers who figure in the ballad are variously given as Tommy Brown, Jimmy Brown, or just Brown for the first man; Jack Murphy, Jack Williams, or Martin, for the second man; and Paul Jones or 'poor Joe' for the third man. And their place of origin is given, in different versions, as Liverpool, Nottingham, Galloway Town and Nenagh Town.

This is one of the versions, usually sung slowly and without accompaniment to convey an atmosphere of stark horror:

'You ramblin' lads of Liverpool, I'd have you all
    beware
When you go out poachin' with your gun, your dog,
    your snare
Take care of the gamekeeper, stand ready for his
    command
Oh, think of hardships undergone, upon Van
    Diemen's Land.

There was Jimmy Brown from Nenagh Town, Jack
    Murphy and poor Joe
We was three darin' poachers, as the country well
    does know
By the keeper of the watch, brave boys, one night we
    were trepanned
And for fourteen years transported unto Van
    Diemen's Land

The ship that bore us from the land, the Speedwell
    was her name
For full four months and a half we ploughed across
    the ragin' main
No land or harbor could we see, and believe me 'tis
    no lie
All around us one black water, all above us one blue
    sky

The moment that we landed upon that fatal shore
The planters they all gathered round, some forty
    score or more
They ranked us up like horses, and they sold us out
    of hand
Then they yoked us to the plough, brave boys, to
    plough Van Diemen's Land

The hovels that we shelter in are built of mud and
    clay
With rotten straw for bedding, and we dare not say
    nay

They fence us in with fire, and we slumber when we can
And we drive off wolves and tigers upon Van Diemen's Land

Last night as I lay sleeping, I had a pleasant dream
With my own sweet girl beside me, down by some purling stream
I was roamin' through old Ireland, with my true love by the hand
But I woke up broken-hearted, lyin' on Van Diemen's Land

God bless our wives and families, likewise that happy shore
That isle of sweet contentment which we shall see no more
As for our wretched females, see them we seldom can
There's twenty to one woman, upon Van Diemen's Land

So all you jolly poachers, come listen to my song
It is a bit of good advice, although it is not long
Lay aside your guns and snares, to you I will speak plain
If you knew the miseries we endure, you'd never poach again.'

This is a conventional transportation ballad, following, as they usually did, a fixed sequence of events — the crime, the sentence, the voyage out, the hardship of convict life, the lament for families at home, and, finally, the warning to others to avoid this dreadful fate.

Obviously, this song is written from a male point of view, but another transportation ballad of about the same time tells a similar story from the female side:

'Sarah Collins is my name, most dreadful is my fate
My father reared me tenderly, the truth I do relate
Till enticed by bad company, along with many a more
It led to my discovery, upon my native shore

My trial it approached fast, before the judge I stood
And when the judge passed sentence, it fairly chilled my blood
Crying, you must be transported for fourteen years or more
Depart from hence across the seas unto Van Diemen's Shore

It hurt my heart when on the coach I my native town passed by
To see so many I did know, it made me heave a sigh

Then to a ship was sent with speed along with many more
Whose aching hearts did grieve to go unto Van Diemen's Shore

The sea was rough, ran mountains high, with us poor girls 'twas hard
No one but God to us came nigh, no one did us regard
At length, alas, we reached the land, it grieved us ten times more
That wretched place Van Diemen's Land, far from our native shore

They chained us two by two, we were whipped and lashed along
They cut off our provisions if we did the least thing wrong
They march us in the burning sun until our feet are raw
So hard's our lot, now we are got unto Van Diemen's Shore

We labor hard from morn to night until our bones do ache
Then everyone they must obey, their mouldy bed must make
We often wish when we lay down we'd never rise no more
To meet our savage governor upon Van Diemen's Shore.'

It could not be said that these ballads overstated the wretchedness of convict life in Van Diemen's Land. It is true that convicts were ranked up like horses and some were actually yoked to ploughs. In any other comparison between horses and convicts, the horses generally came off best. They were well fed and treated as creatures of some value. They were not strapped to the triangles at the whim of some officer, nor were they brutally flogged until their backbones were bared to the chill Tasmanian air.

But there was little pity wasted on the convicts by the respectable citizens of their own day — that kind of sentiment only came later, when Australia developed a sense of conscience, rather than a habit of reticence, about its past. A Mr David Burn, who inspected Port Arthur in 1842, and wrote an account of his trip in the *Tasmanian Journal,* was impressed by every aspect of the settlement except the convicts themselves:

'Next day being Sunday, we proceeded after breakfast to see the convicts mustered prior to their being marched to church. They were drawn up in three lines, each gang forming a separated division — the overseers (convicts) taking their stations in the rear. It was hideous to remark the countenances of the men, to which their yellow raiment (or half black, half yellow) with P.A. and their respective numbers stamped on various parts, imparted a sinister and most revolting expression. Scarcely one open set of features was to be found. To read their eyes, it seemed as though they were speculating the chance of gain or advantage to be hoped from us. Crime and its consequences were fearfully depicted in their visages; and we turned from the disagreeable caricature of humanity with as much disgust as pity and regret.'

Burn inspected the accommodation, tasted the food and pronounced both excellent; too good,

perhaps, for criminal wretches who were enjoying better lives and conditions than many a starving British labourer.

To us, such judgements sound harsh and unfeeling. Yet it is true that Port Arthur was not the worst of the convict settlements. Moreton Bay was worse, and Norfolk Island was infinitely worse. A convict's life was never roses, but Van Diemen's Land, throughout most of its area and throughout most of its time as a penal colony, was not a convict hell. Its reputation as a land of horror, and as a name that struck a chill into the heart of every convicted felon, rested entirely on one small and remote settlement, which existed for only eleven years.

This settlement was within a vast harbour, halfway up the wild western coast of Tasmania where the great rollers of the Southern Ocean break against the rocks and the icy blasts from the South Pole lash the Huon pine forests. The harbour was discovered in 1815 by a colonial sea captain, James Kelly. Captain Kelly was a noted character, somewhat larger than life in more ways than one. It was said that his trousers, when he himself was not occupying

below: **Ruins of Courthouse, Settlement Island**

them, were so capacious that they could contain two jumbo-sized sacks of flour. Kelly named this huge harbour Macquarie Harbour. It was intended as an honour to the Governor, but the subsequent events at Macquarie Harbour dishonoured the name of a man who did much to give convicts a vision of hope in a country that others still regarded strictly as a gaol. Captain Kelly named other features of the harbour, including Liberty Point, Sarah Island and the Gordon River, and he noted that a fine tree, the Huon pine, grew on the banks of the harbour. Two mountains that loomed in the hinterland had already been named, by Flinders in 1798, Mount Heemskerk and Mount Zeehan, for the ships of Abel Tasman. These mountains were the high points of land that gave Tasman his first sight from the ocean of Van Diemen's Land.

The most appropriate name at Macquarie Harbour was not bestowed by Captain Kelly. The entrance to the harbour became known as Hell's Gates. The origin of the name is uncertain. It may have been given by sailors because of the dangerous character of the narrow strait, or it may have been given by convicts. Certainly, it was for convicts that the name held a dire meaning because the entrance to Macquarie Harbour did indeed become a gateway to Hell. Within that storm-beaten harbour was the most terrible prison of its time, a place worse than Devil's Island, a place comparable in horror to the Nazi concentration camps of Buchenwald and Belsen. There was no single and terrible revelation of what had gone on at Macquarie Harbour, as there was at Buchenwald and Belsen. But as the story of Macquarie Harbour gradually emerged, men found it difficult to believe that other men, creatures of the same flesh and blood, could be capable of the atrocities that were committed there.

Kelly's mention of the Huon pines created interest in Hobart and there were several exploratory logging trips to Macquarie Harbour before 1821 when Lieutenant-Governor Sorell had the idea of using the harbour for an additional purpose. The first convict settlement at Norfolk Island had been

below: **Settlement Island, formerly Sarah Island, a convict's hell**

closed down seven years earlier and the convicts had been brought to Van Diemen's Land. Sorell faced the problem of what to do with recalcitrant prisoners, re-convicted felons and habitual offenders, and it occurred to him that such scum could be employed usefully in felling the Huon pine on the west coast. But Macquarie Harbour was a fearfully remote place, even in the comparatively small island of Van Diemen's Land. An apparently impenetrable chain of mountains blocked access by land, and it could only be reached by sea on a dangerous voyage below the island and through the stormy waters of the south-west passage.

It was not, therefore, the most ideal place to begin a logging operation. But that was not the chief consideration in Sorell's mind. When, in June 1821, he recommended 'the formation of a small establishment at Macquarie Harbour on the West Coast of this Island as a Place of ultra banishment and punishment of convicts for which the valuable products of that spot seem to render it so well adapted', it was the ultra banishment and punishment of convicts that was foremost in his mind. He considered that there had to be an ultimate deterrent in prisons; a place so fearful that even the most desperate of convict rogues would not risk being sent there. Macquarie Harbour was chosen as the place.

Sorell's successor, Governor Arthur, initially shared his views and in 1824 issued these instructions to the Commandant of Macquarie Harbour:

'You will consider that the constant, active, unremitting employment of every individual convict in very hard labour is the general and main design of your settlement. Banishment to Macquarie Harbour must be considered by the whole class of convicts a place of such strict discipline that they must dread the very idea of being sent there. Let your discipline be seasoned with humanity but never lose sight of a continued, rigid, unrelaxing discipline, and you must find work and labour, even if it consists of opening cavities and filling them up again . . . Prisoners upon trial declared they would rather suffer death than be sent back to

Macquarie Harbour, which is proof that banishment to that station operates as it is intended. It is the feeling I am most anxious to keep alive.'

Throughout the years of the Macquarie Harbour prison, from 1822 to 1833, the gaolers observed these instructions almost to the letter. Where they departed from the letter was in not bothering to season their discipline with humanity. Marcus Clarke made Macquarie Harbour the location for his *For the Term of His Natural Life,* and his description of the conditions there was authentic in every detail:

'The military force numbered about sixty men, who, with convict workers and constables, took charge of more than three hundred and fifty prisoners. These miserable wretches, deprived of every hope, were employed in the most degrading labour. No beast of burden was allowed on the settlement; all the pulling and dragging was done by human beings. . . . The convicts were lodged on Sarah Island, in barracks flanked by a two storied prison, whose "cells" were the terror of the most hardened. Each morning they received their breakfast of porridge, water and salt, and then rowed, under the protection of their guard, to the wood-cutting stations, where they worked without food, until night. The launching and hewing of the timber compelled them to work up to their waists in water. Many of them were heavily ironed.'

Elsewhere, Clarke added:

'Treated like beasts, the men lived the life of beasts. All the atrocities that men could commit were committed there. Suicide was frequent. Men drowned themselves to be rid of the burden of their existence. Three wretches once drew lots as to who should get a sight of Hobart Town. One was to murder the other, and the third was to volunteer his evidence. The lottery was drawn, the doomed man laughed ere his companion beat out his brains, and the two survivors congratulated each other on their holiday on the scaffold of Hobart Town gaol.'

Death was the way of life at Macquarie Harbour. Although there were seldom more than 300 prisoners in the settlement, James Backhouse, a Quaker missionary who visited there, estimated that there had been 85 deaths in 11 years, and of these only 35 had been from 'natural causes': 27 others were drowned, 8 killed accidentally by the falling of trees, 3 shot by the military, and 12 murdered by their companions. In addition, Backhouse reckoned that 112 prisoners had escaped from the settlement and 62 of those had perished in the bush while 9 more had been eaten by their fellow escapees. Backhouse's figures certainly erred on the conservative side. He did not mention the considerable numbers of convicts executed by hanging, both at Macquarie Harbour and at Hobart, nor the number of guards and overseers killed, while the number of convicts eaten by their cannibal companions was at least double the figure he gave.

In addition, the deaths from 'natural causes' must be taken to include the effects of exposure to a dreadful winter climate, starvation diet, confinement in cells three feet wide, and floggings for the most trivial offences, such as being in possession of a potato, or a fish hook, or half an inch of tobacco. One brutal overseer in 1822 spread 7 000 lashes amongst 169 convicts. And they were no ordinary floggings; the sadists who ran the establishment experimented with whips of double-twisted and knotted cords, and with a cat-and-ten-tails, tipped with copper wire.

One especially bestial overseer, Alexander Anderson, had seventeen men flogged in one day. They each got 100 lashes, and any convict who so much as muttered an oath while he was strapped to the triangle, immediately got another 100 lashes. If flogging failed to break a man's spirit, there were other punishments. There was the chain gang, in which sixty convicts were fastened at a time. They were never free of the chain, and had to move like a human centipede, and perform every human action in unison. If a man sat down — or fell down — independently, he jarred the convicts next in line, and ran the risk of being murdered by them on the spot. Some men spent seven years in the chain gang and those that survived walked forever after with an action that suggested that they were still ironed to a file of invisible comrades.

The other extreme sanction at Macquarie Harbour, short of actual execution, was solitary confinement on a rock in the middle of the harbour called Grummet Rock or Condemned Island. It was here that Marcus Clarke had Rufus Dawes, the hero of his novel, confined in irons like a captive wild beast, until he despaired and attempted to commit suicide by throwing himself off the rock. Instead, he was able to make his escape by catching on to a pine log that was floating down the harbour.

Not surprisingly, many convicts in real life attempted to escape from Macquarie Harbour. Some chose the simplest way, death, either by murdering a mate or arranging to have themselves murdered. Others attempted to escape by land. But the harbour had been chosen as a prison because it was hemmed in on three sides by towering mountains and almost impenetrable forests. Most of the convicts who attempted to escape this way perished, and, to this day, skeletons and irons are still being found in the remote bush areas where they died. Those few who survived the overland escape attempts were, in practically every case, recaptured, and it was usually found that they had survived by the most dreadful expedients.

'Price Warung' (William Astley), in his story *Lieutenant Darrell's Predicament,* gave this account of one escapee:

'A convict who had escaped from the settlement at Sarah Island in company with seven others, returned alone, five weeks later. He had, he reported, lost his companions ten days after the escape, and had sustained life in the interval on wild berries, fish caught in the streams, and the pith of the grass-tree. His plump appearance gave the lie to his story, and a certain slavering of the mouth left those familiar with the annals of Hell's Gates (which, though few, were already full of indescribable ghastlinesses) no doubt whatever as to the means by which he had succeeded in maintaining his physical vigour. He was accordingly given his choice as to whether he would be hanged there and then as an absconder, or be first flogged for "absenting himself from work" and then be sent to Hobart Town to be tried (and hanged) for the murder of his fellow-

above: **Denuded hills at Queenstown**

left: **Devastated bank of King River**

escapees. Naturally, the wretch preferred the latter course. Death was equally certain in either case, but the Hobart Town trip offered the supreme enjoyment of a change of scene, and a glass of hot spirit the night before execution.'

This description — and also the hideous character, Gabbett, in *For the Term of his Natural Life* — referred to an actual convict, Alexander Pierce. Pierce escaped *twice* from Macquarie Harbour. On his first escape in 1822, during the first year of the prison settlement, he was accompanied by seven other convicts. After eight days in the bush they were starving, and a victim, Alexander Dalton, was axed to death, cooked on a fire and eaten. The rest of the party successively met the same fate until only Pierce and the other ringleader, Bob Greenhill, were left. Greenhill had been the chief executioner and had insisted on keeping possession of the axe. But ultimately, as the two men glared at each other across a camp fire, Greenhill lost the battle to stay awake. The moment he dozed off, Pierce snatched the axe from his hand, killed him, and ate him. With this supply of meat, Pierce actually managed to reach the eastern side of the ranges, an achievement no other man had accomplished, on foot from Macquarie Harbour. He fell in with a gang of sheepstealers, was captured with them and sent back to Macquarie Harbour.

At this stage, he was treated merely as a bolter. It was not known that he had already eaten seven men. But, in 1823, Pierce persuaded another convict, called Cox, to make an escape attempt with him. They struck northwards along the coast from Macquarie Harbour. Five days later, Pierce was observed signalling from the shore, by the ship *Waterloo*, and was picked up. According to some accounts, Pierce signalled to the ship by waving one of Cox's bones, with flesh still clinging to it. Hunks of half-eaten meat from Cox's body were found in his pockets. Before his execution, Pierce confessed his dreadful story. He had become demented with a craze for human flesh and he stated that he much preferred its flavour to pork, chicken or fish.

This became the most notorious incident of cannibalism at Macquarie Harbour, but there were others scarcely less horrible. Charles Routley, who escaped from the prison in 1830, murdered six men and roasted one of the bodies, wrapped in a bullock skin, and ate it. Captured and brought to trial in Hobart, he brandished the iron hook that he had in place of a chopped-off hand, and damned the judge and the court in most blasphemous terms. Before his hanging, he made a show of contrition, and whimpered to the chaplain 'Oh, Mr Bedford, what is to become of me?'.

The question the court should have asked, but didn't, was what had happened to men like Pierce and Routley to make them become what they were. However wicked the convicts sent to Macquarie Harbour may have been, the treatment they received there could only bring them to despair or desperation. In the first five years, one out of every two convicts tried to escape. Only a desperate man would have attempted to escape from the prison by land. Those with a vestige of sanity left were able to calculate that their only chance lay in escape by sea. And there were three such attempts that succeeded, at least for a time.

The first was led by Matthew Brady, for a short time Van Diemen Land's most notorious bushranger. Brady, with a party of twelve men, seized a ship's whaleboat and navigated it through the perilous waters to the south and east until they reached the Derwent. There Brady and a band of followers took to the bush where they operated with much audacity, on one occasion capturing the entire village of Sorell. When Governor Arthur issued a proclamation in 1825 offering a reward of twenty-five guineas for Brady's capture, the bushranger replied with his own proclamation, which he posted outside an inn.

'Mountain Home, April 20, 1825
It has caused Matthew Brady much concern that such a person known as Sir George Arthur is at large. Twenty gallons of rum will be given to any person that will deliver his person unto me. I also caution John Priest that I will hang him for his ill-treatment of Mrs Blackwell, at Newton.
M. Brady.'

Brady finally surrendered to a party led by John Batman in 1826. The reputation he had gained for gallantry, and the numerous petitions from his fair admirers, were insufficient to save him from the gallows at Hobart Town.

If Macquarie Harbour achieved anything positive, it was in the building of fifteen quite respectable ships at the yards on Sarah Island. Two of these ships figured in convict escapes, which was appropriate enough, since the prisoners had built them. In 1829, the Government brig *Cyprus*, bound for Macquarie Harbour with a cargo of thirty-one convicts, was seized by the convicts at Recherche Bay and sailed away into the Pacific. The incident excited considerable interest both in the Australian colonies and in Britain. It became the subject of a play and of this folksong, *The Cyprus Brig*, written some years afterwards in Tasmania by a convict sympathiser:

*Poor Tom Brown from Nottingham, Jack Williams and poor Joe
They were three gallant poacher boys, their country all does know*

And by the laws of Amalgamac, that you may understand
Were fourteen years transported, boys, unto Van Diemen's Land.

When we landed in this colony, to different masters went,
For trifling offences, boys, to Hobart gaol were sent.
Now the second sentence we received, and ordered for to be
Sent to Macquarie Harbour, that place of tyranny.

Down Hobart streets were guarded, on the Cyprus Brig conveyed
Our topsails they were hoisted, boys, our anchor it was weighed
The wind it blew a nor-nor-west, and on we steered straight way
Till we brought her to an anchorage in a place called Research Bay

Now confined in a dismal hole, those lads contrived a plan
To take possession of that Brig, or else die every man
The plan it being approved upon, we all retired to rest
And early the next morning, boys, we put them to the test

Up steps bold Jack Moldamon, his comrades three or more,
We soon disarmed the sentry and left him in his gore.
It's Liberty, O Liberty, it's Liberty we crave,
Deliver up your arms, my boys, or the sea shall be your grave.

First we landed the soldiers, the captain and his crew
We gave three cheers for Liberty, and soon bid them adieu.
William Swallow he was chosen our commander for to be
We gave three cheers for Liberty, and boldly put to sea'

Although strands of other old songs, such as *Van Diemen's Land* and *Bold Jack Donahoe*, are woven into the ballad *The Cyprus Brig*, the story it tells is broadly true. The convicts seized the

top: **Queenstown, headquarters of Mount Lyell Mines**

left: **Arch Edwards at Tasmanian Smelter, Zeehan**

ship while the commander, Lieutenant Carew, was absent with a fishing party. They marooned Carew, his family and the soldiers and sailors, on the shore of Recherche Bay, together with thirteen prisoners who refused to join the plot. They left them a small supply of provisions and most of these forty-five castaways were rescued a fortnight later. Meanwhile, the rebel convicts, eighteen in number, sailed the ship away, with a large supply of provisions that had been intended for the prison settlement. Their leader, William Swallow, was a former seaman who had already escaped once from Van Diemen's Land as a stowaway, been captured in Rio de Janiero, escaped again, been recaptured in London and sent back to Van Diemen's Land.

With Swallow as navigator, the *Cyprus* headed into the South Seas. It was assumed in the colony that she was bound for Valparaiso, but Swallow sailed the brig to Tahiti, where seven of the convicts jumped ship, and then to Japan, where he scuttled the ship. He and three companions next turned up in Canton, where, under assumed names, they talked their way into free passages to England.

The song of the *Cyprus Brig* ends on a stirring note of liberty, but, in fact, nearly all of the escapees were recaptured and either locked up or executed. Swallow himself was retaken by a desperately unlucky chance, when he was recognised in a London street, and arrested on a charge of piracy. He was transported once again to Van Diemen's Land and died in chains at Port Arthur. By then, the Macquarie Harbour convict hell had been abandoned, but not because of any official contrition for the worst atrocities ever perpetrated by the Australian penal system. It was closed down because it was too inconvenient to keep it open. It was dangerous to reach and difficult to supply and, by 1833, even the warders had had enough. Few men were anxious to be assigned to guard-duty at such a desolate place.

The curtain on Macquarie Harbour's penal history came down with a very appropriate crash. The brig *Frederick* was assigned to sail from the harbour on January 11, 1834, taking

away to Hobart anything that was considered worth taking, including the doors and windows from the prison buildings and the last four soldiers and the last ten convicts. But the last convict ship to leave Macquarie Harbour was detained by adverse winds and two of the soldiers repeated the fatal mistake that had lost the *Cyprus* — they went off fishing. The convicts seized control of the ship and marooned the soldiers, the shipwright and the pilot. To save themselves, this party had to struggle northwards through the wild bush to the Van Diemen's Land Company's settlement at Circular Head, on Bass Strait.

Meanwhile, the *Frederick,* under the doubtful navigation of a convict named John Barker, set sail across the Pacific. Six weeks later the leaking vessel just managed to get them to the coast of Chile. They applied for refuge to the Spanish governor in Valdivia and were permitted to remain, and several of them got married. But, a year later, a new governor agreed to hand them over to a British ship that came into the port. Six of the convicts disappeared and were never heard of again.

right: **Church at Zeehan**

131

The other four ended their days under life sentences at the new 'place of ultra banishment', Norfolk Island.

At Macquarie Harbour, the prison ruins crumbled away for the next half century, unseen and unvisited except by a handful of loggers who came on seasonal trips to gather the valuable Huon pine which still grew in profusion on the Gordon River. The tremendous quality of this timber had been recognised since at least 1810 when it was paid this somewhat morbid tribute in the *Derwent Star*:

> 'It must afford a melancholy satisfaction to the relatives and friends of our late Lieutenant-Governor (Davey) to know that the body was placed in a shell of Huon pine which is impenetrable to the worm.'

However, it was not the timber but the minerals in the earth beneath that brought the rush of civilisation to the West Coast of Tasmania. In 1871 a prospector called 'Philosopher Smith' discovered tin at Mount Bischoff. Within the next twenty years gold was discovered at the Pieman River, silver at Waratah, Zeehan, Dundas and Farrell, copper at Mount Lyell, tin at Renison Bell, and zinc-lead sulphide at Rosebery.

When Tasman, in the *Zeehan*, had sailed by the mountain later named for his ship, his compass had gone crazy. He did not understand why, but the reason became apparent two and a half centuries later. The mountains of Western Tasmania were chock-full of rich minerals. In the last quarter of the nineteenth century, Tasmania's population increased by half as much again and its prosperity increased five times over because of the West Coast mines. *The Australian Mining Standard* crowed: 'We cannot remember any period in the history of these colonies when discovery after discovery of undoubted value followed each other so quickly.'

In 1882, a miner named Frank Long discovered an outcrop of rich galena (silver-lead ore) on the bank of a muddy little stream called Pea Soup Creek. Like most discoverers of mining fields in Australia, Long did not become rich from his find, but others did and the boom town of Zeehan sprang up near the site of his find. When a railway line was built in 1890 between Zeehan and the port of Strahan, on Macquarie Harbour, the boom could be heard around the world, and immigrants rushed to the new bonanza. During the next twenty years, the population of Zeehan reached 10 000, making it the third largest metropolis in Tasmania. There were 159 mines and syndicates working in the area, and mines like the Silver Queen, the Western and the Montana employed thousands of men and produced in their peak years more than seven million dollars worth of silver.

Zeehan itself was called 'The Silver City' and 'The Capital of the West Coast'. It was a noisy, rip-roaring place where the blasts of the mine whistles mingled with the clatter of the trams down the centre of the main street and the hissing of the steam engines at the huge marshalling yards. Eleven different railway companies operated into Zeehan on an amazing variety of gauges including the remarkable Abt railway, which had a third track in the middle and was designed for pulling heavy loads up mountainous grades. Mountainous was a mild word for the grades on which some of these lines operated: the West Coast mining lines involved some quite hair-raising feats of railway engineering.

At its height, around 1908, Zeehan boasted twenty-six pubs, a spectacular variety of shops and Australia's largest legitimate theatre, the Gaiety. Tommy Burns, the world heavyweight boxing champion, gave a sparring exhibition in the theatre in that year and the crowds turned up in thousands, though some say it was not to see Tommy, but his motor car, which was freighted in by rail and was the first ever seen in Zeehan. At that time, and for many years afterwards, Zeehan's only communication links were by rail, to the north coast, and to the southern port of Strahan.

Local legend has it that the Gaiety featured more stars than there were in the heavens. Names like Enrico Caruso, Nellie Stewart, Lola Montez, Madam Melba, Blondin, Houdini — practically every famous name in theatre is claimed to have appeared there except William Shakespeare, but even he was there in spirit. His bust still gazes from the top of the stage though it no longer has an audience to inspect or a box-office take to calculate.

Some of the claimed appearances are impossible; others are difficult to establish. There is a lively controversy as to whether Madam Melba played the Gaiety. The suggestion that Melba *intended* to appear at the Gaiety, but couldn't, because she got drunk on the train, still raises the hackles of Melba fans, who insist that she was abstemious at all times. What is certain is that many of J. C. Williamson's theatre companies appeared at the Gaiety, before audiences of a thousand boisterous miners and their families. Other acts seen on the stage included prize fighters, wood choppers, and a performing horse, who was followed around the stage by a man with a shovel. Perhaps the horse was an early theatre critic.

Later, when movies were introduced, the Gaiety became a picture theatre and it competed against its local rival, the Royal, with advertising stunts, brass bands out in the streets, search-lights lighting up the sky — all the hooray of Hollywood. It even advertised a 'talkie', twenty years before Hollywood had them. The 'talkie' turned out to be a 'singie' — a film of a man opening and shutting his mouth, accompanied by a gramophone record played from the projection box. The fans were not annoyed by this innocent deception. On the contrary, they were overwhelmed by the sheer magic of it all.

Today the Royal has long gone. The Gaiety can still be seen at Zeehan — it's now a recreation hall for a mining company — and so can the Grand Hotel, the School of Mines, and the Railway Museum, where one can inspect the locomotives that operated on railway lines now extinct.

Zeehan's boom ended when the smelter closed down at the start of the Great War. Some mining continued until 1960, when the last local mine, the Oceana, ceased to operate, but through the years, as jobs became scarcer, the glow of the smelter that had once lit the night sky was replaced by a different kind of glow. Half the houses in Zeehan burned down. Many were allegedly ignited by their owners to collect the insurance money — perhaps the only way that a bankrupt family could raise the money to pay its debts and get out of a dying town. It is said that the fires were so frequent that fashionable ladies went in for expensive nightwear so as to make a sudden and impressive appearance at the latest conflagration.

Whole streets of old Zeehan have disappeared and though the town has recently had a new lease of life, through being used as a housing base for the nearby Renison Bell mines, it is not easy now to recapture the atmosphere that Zeehan enjoyed in its boom days.

Nor is it easy to picture the sleeping little town of Strahan, on Macquarie Harbour, as Australia's most important port. But in the years 1901 and 1902, the value of the cargo that passed through Strahan was greater than that of any other port in Australia. The mining produce of the West was railed into the town and it was as well the passenger port for the entire coast with weekly services to Hobart, Launceston and Melbourne. Strahan is still the only port on the West Coast, but there's not much call for its services now. Apart from fishing, the town's chief business is tourism. During the summer months, the *Denison Star* carries hundreds of tourists on cruises of Macquarie Harbour and the Gordon River. The Gordon is still the only way into some of Australia's wildest country and the scenery in the steep gorges of Tasmania's most powerful river is quite sensational.

There are aspects of Macquarie Harbour that don't bear too close an examination. The King River, for instance, has been turned into a stream of cement, having been used for years as a tip for the industrial waste of Mount Lyell Mines and the human waste of Queenstown. Some locals are worried that the beauty of the Gordon River might also be drowned by proposed hydro-electric dams. But, in summer, Macquarie Harbour is still one of the most beautiful and unspoilt places in Australia. In winter, it is a different proposition, lashed by driving rain and the howling gales of the Roaring Forties. These were the conditions the convicts knew and dreaded; and, unlike tourists, they didn't have the option of wintering somewhere else.

To visit Sarah Island, even today, is a sobering experience. It is now called Settlement Island, but there is no settlement there. The bush has taken over and only a few traces can

above: **Stately old home at Strahan**

opposite: **Tree ferns, Dandenongs**

be seen of the convict prison cells and the shipyards by the shore. The most prominent ruin is the Court of Justice, a wrecked edifice which is a suitable monument to a system that wrecked all human values. In the words of the early Tasmanian historian, John West:

> 'The name of Macquarie Harbour is associated exclusively with remembrance of impossible depravity, degradation and woe. Sacred to the genius of torture, nature concurred with the objects of its separation from the rest of the world, to exhibit some notion of a perfect misery. There, man lost the aspect and the heart of man!'

There is still on this island an atmosphere of brooding melancholy especially at nightfall, when the mountain walls, which were the convicts' *prison* walls, loom in the distance. You can almost hear through the shadows those ancient cries of fear and agony, and the images of Rex Ingamells' *Macquarie Harbour* strike home:

> 'Macquarie Harbour jailers lock
> the sullen gates no more
> but lash-strokes sound in every shock
> of ocean on the dismal rock
> along that barren shore
>
> No more the bolters hear the hound
> that brays upon the wind,
> and terror-spurred keep onward bound
> until they drop upon the ground
> starved and terror-pinned . . .
>
> but gales that whine among the hills
> sniff at the savage tracks
> the hopeless took. The snowfall fills
> bleak ranges; then the moonlight spills
> broad arrows on their backs.'

THE DANDENONGS

Melbourne was founded in 1835 by parties of settlers from Van Diemen's Land, led by John Batman and John Pascoe Fawkner. The settlement was not at first called Melbourne. It was variously known as Batmania, Glenelg, Bearbrass, Bearport, Bareheap or Bearbury. The names beginning with 'Bear' were all derived from the Aboriginal name for the locality, which was Berrern, or Bararing.

In 1837, Governor Bourke bestowed the name of Melbourne on the settlement in honour of the British Prime Minister. No doubt Bourke reckoned that he knew what he was doing. But it is a pity, in a way, that he chose to plant yet another British politician's name on the map when the names already in use offered such delightful possibilities. I think it could be amusing if one of Australia's great capital cities of the present day was known as Batmania, or even as Bareheap (although I would not expect this notion to find much favour in the more dignified quarters of Melbourne).

The settlement was founded on a bare coastal plain, with no inspiring natural scenery in the immediate area. However, there was clearly visible, twenty miles to the east of the village on the Yarra, a beautiful range of blue mountains. Melbourne fixed its collective gaze on these mountains, and has kept it there ever since. The range was the hunting-grounds of the Wurundjeri, a group of the Kulin nation which inhabited south-eastern and central Victoria. The tallest peak of the range was known to the Wurundjeri as Tanjenong, meaning 'very high' or possibly 'burning bush'. (Summer bushfires on that mountain were frequent and fierce, as white men later discovered to their cost.) They called the other prominent peak Corhanwarrabul, meaning 'a desirable and attractive place, replete with birds flying, kangaroos jumping, and lyrebirds singing'. One can only deduce that the Wurundjeri were not a people to waste words. However, their one-word description of the mountain was both accurate and comprehensive. Corhanwarrabul was also the name that the Aborigines gave to the entire range, but the white settlers named the range for the higher peak, and for once, they stuck to the native name, although it was changed in their

pronunciation from Tanjenong to Dandenong. It was soon estimated that Mount Dandenong was 2 078 feet high and the other mountain, whose name became spelt as Corranwarrabul, was 2 050 feet high.

The Dandenongs, where the tribes had hunted in the summer months for wallaby, possum and native bear, were quickly put into use as grazing runs. The Reverend James Clow took up Corhanwarrabul Run in 1838, and ran cattle over an area of thirty-six square miles. Joseph Hawdon, the famous overlander, soon afterwards took up the Dandenong run and a number of other white settlers also took up stations in the area.

The first naturalist to be attracted by the evident beauty and variety of this region was Daniel Bunce, a botanist, who arrived from Hobart in 1839. A couple of years later, he ascended Mount Corranwarrabul in the company of Aboriginal guides and made notes on the plant life. Bunce recorded that 'the short, rich notes of the native thrush, the sweet warble of the magpie and the jocund cadence of the laughing jackass reverberated through the woods'. He also heard the marvellous lyre-bird, which can imitate any noise, from a drunken party to a cross-cut saw, and he remarked on 'the ridiculous sounds of mimicry raised by this Australian mocking bird'.

Victoria's most renowned naturalist, Baron Ferdinand von Mueller, paid a week's visit to the Dandenongs in 1853, soon after he had been appointed Government Botanist. His companion, John Walters, reported:

'On reaching the summit, we beheld some of the finest timber trees which it is possible to have any idea of; three quarters had, however, a charred appearance and were comparatively leafless, being thus destroyed by an extensive bush fire, which about two years ago swept over nearly the whole country . . . All the bark was hanging loosely from the lifeless tree in strips like ropes from the top of some huge tree of liberty.'

But, by now, a more regular and efficient destroyer of trees than the bushfire had arrived on the scene. Naturalists were not the only men to notice the huge stands of timber in the Dandenongs. The eyes and the axes of the timbergetters fell particularly on the giant mountain ash, *Eucalyptus regnans*, and many of these noble trees were felled and dragged away to build the wharves and piers and bridges of the expanding city of Melbourne.

The mountain ash is the tallest species of eucalyptus, and the tallest hardwood tree in the world. Its name signifies 'the king of trees'. Californians might be inclined to dispute that title nowadays, and point to the Founders Redwood in their Redwood Forest which is 364 feet high and still standing. But there is a record of a Dandenongs mountain ash which was measured a century ago at 375 feet. Unfortunately, it was measured lying on the ground, after it had been chopped down. The trees that can now be seen in places like Sherbrooke Forest are no higher than 300 feet — which, of course, is still no mean height for a tree. The timbercutters went straight for the tallest specimens, even if they had to hack down acres of scrub to get them, and an area that had evolved as virgin forest for a million years lost its noblest specimens in a space of about twenty years.

Reports of this fine timber spread far and wide and one man particularly interested in the news was a Captain John Freyer, who sailed into Port Phillip Bay in 1850 with two of the masts of his barque *Admiral* snapped by storms on the voyage from Glasgow. Freyer headed for the Dandenongs to find replacements, and was delighted to find, in the area of Upway, what he described as 'a forest of ships masts'. He had two spars cut out, each 100 feet long and over 2 feet thick, and he engaged four bullock teams to drag them back to port.

It took twenty-six bullocks to haul just one of these masts through the rough ranges and it was six weeks after the *Admiral* had anchored in the bay the first mast was delivered. When the bullockies went back to get the second mast, which they'd left beside the track at Ferntree Gully, they discovered that somebody with a peculiar sense of humour had neatly cut the giant spar in two. So it then took them another month to cut and transport a third mast. The place where the trees were felled is known today as Mast Gully Creek.

The mountain ash was not the only natural growth to suffer from these onslaughts. Early settlers and visitors in the Dandenongs recorded lush growth of white gum, blackwood, sassafras, beech, dogwood and musk trees, as well as magnificent specimens of tree ferns, some of them thirty feet high. But there were no official moves to declare the area a timber reserve until 1867 when the Victorian Government instructed John Hardy to survey the area for declaration as a State Forest. On April 1, 1867, an area of 26 500 acres on the summit of the Dandenong Ranges was declared 'The Dandenong and Woori Yallock State Forest'. The date of the official declaration, April Fool's Day, was probably significant as within two years the Government passed another Act giving itself the power to revoke any previous proclamation of a timber reserve by the simple expedient of giving one month's notice in the *Government Gazette*.

By this time, the tallest trees had already disappeared from the mountains and other damage had been done, but the Dandenong Ranges was still a comparatively wild area, sparsely populated by timbergetters in their ramshackle camps, and by pastoralists who held only lease-hold rights to the land.

There had been a temporary surge of population in 1858 when gold was discovered at Emerald and a thousand miners rushed to the 'Dandenong Goldfield'. But the Australian miner, while he believed in going anywhere for gold, also believed in pulling out quickly if he couldn't find any. Within a year the population at Emerald was down to three hundred. Within two years it was down to fifty. In a country where half the mountains seemed to be bulging with minerals, the Dandenongs offered no chance of gaining a quick fortune that way. But there were other riches in these mountains. The lush growth of trees and plants was supported by an average rainfall of fifty inches a year and a volcanic soil that was as good as the best in Australia. It looked as if it was capable of growing anything, and, in time, it turned out to be.

The Dandenong Range's greatest advantage, and at the same time its greatest problem, has always been its proximity to Melbourne. Within eleven years of the proclamation of the Dandenong State Forest in 1867, Melbourne's demand for land and living space had become so strong that the Victorian Government declared 10 000 acres of the forest open for selection and private sale. With one stroke of the pen, the infant State Forest was reduced to three-fifths of its original size, and the chance to preserve the whole range as a natural forest heritage was lost.

However, the Government had to deal with circumstances as they saw them, and ecology (a word they'd never heard of) filled no empty bellies and won no votes. The new selection areas, on the fringes and foothills of the originally proclaimed State Forest, were soon occupied by small farmers who cleared the trees and natural vegetation, and planted crops of raspberries, apples and vegetables. The areas from Menzies Creek to Upper Ferntree Gully in the south, and in the Basin and Ferny Creek and One Tree Hill to the north, became market gardens to feed the hungry city.

A severe depression overtook Victoria in the 1890s and the produce of the Dandenongs was not much use then to the city battlers of Fitzroy and Collingwood who had no jobs and consequently no money to pay for food, or even to pay the rent.

John McIntyre, the Minister for Lands, conceived, or misconceived, a scheme to rescue the starving poor of Melbourne by settling them on ten-acre blocks of land, where they would theoretically become self-supporting. As part of this plan, a further 10 000 acres was carved out of the Dandenongs State Forest by a proclamation of 1893. The forest was now reduced to one-fifth of its original size, a fairly remarkable rate of diminution in a period of just twenty-six years.

For those people who would have wished, then or now, that the Dandenongs should be preserved as a single coherent area of native mountain bushland, the consequences of McIntyre's scheme were much worse than those of the 1878 land grab.

That early scheme had diminished the size of the Dandenong State Forest but had left its heartland intact. Under McIntyre's plan, the highest ridges and most picturesque slopes of

below: **Tom Brown, old time coachman**

the Dandenongs were thrown open for settlement. Even in 1893, which was not exactly the peak year of the bush conservation movement, there was considerable criticism of the Minister's brainwave. It was pointed out that the steep and heavily timbered gorges of the Dandenongs, while very beautiful and grand to look at, were not the most ideal spots to plant poor and inexperienced settlers.

But the plan proceeded. The destruction of some of the most beautiful places in the Dandenongs was achieved at a high cost to posterity, and also to the settlers themselves. Two classes of people were allowed to take up land under the conditions of the *McIntyre Act*. 'Village Settlers' were granted some financial aid by the Government. 'Free Selectors' were expected to depend on their own resources. Both classes were permitted to take up blocks of ten acres, on condition that they cleared the

below: **The Mountain Ash, King of The Dandenongs**

below right: **Olde English cuisine, The Baron of Beef, Sherbrooke**

land. Farms, and the beginnings of rough village settlements, sprang up at Monbulk, Scoresby, Tremont, the Patch, Fairy Dell, Sassafras, Olinda, Kallista and Sherbrooke. The settlers had a very rough time of it. Most of them had little money and no bush experience. A good many decided that life in the forest was too harsh and primitive and that the task of clearing the timber was beyond them. Within a couple of years they had battled their way back to the seedy but familiar slums of inner Melbourne.

Those that remained first of all had to create some kind of log-cabin dwelling for their families, and then get on with the back-breaking task of clearing the bush. They often had to get 150 trees off one acre of land. Even after they'd done this, they found that the ten-acre blocks were too small to provide a decent livelihood. They really needed blocks of fifty acres or more. All they could do with ten-acre blocks was turn them into gardens, after they'd gained whatever money they could from selling the timber they'd felled.

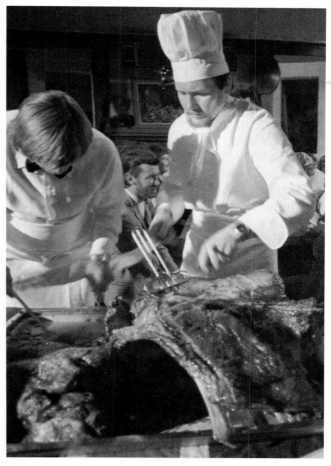

They grew fruit and vegetable crops, chiefly gooseberries, raspberries, strawberries and cabbages, and they found this no great task in the Dandenongs because of the rich soil and high rainfall. The real problem was getting their produce to market. There were no made roads in the area when they arrived, only rough bullock tracks. The settlers had to hack out their own roads to reach the railhead at Upper Ferntree Gully, and even after horse-drawn coach services started up, the roads were often too slippery to negotiate in winter.

The village settlers, who had no great financial stake in their holdings, were the ones who tended to walk off, especially after the Government aid cut out. The free selectors, who'd invested their life savings in their properties, hung on like grim death. But the depression was still on and prices were low. They made meagre returns from their produce if they took it to market themselves, and no profit at all if they had to commission other people to take it to market. Some of the free selectors had been lucky enough to retain jobs in the city. At the same time, the terms under which they took up land in the Dandenongs required them to live on their selections. Their solution was to walk to Ferntree Gully every Sunday night and catch the train to Melbourne. There these men worked through the week, sleeping in the cheapest residentials and boarding-houses they could find. On Friday night they caught the train back to the mountains with a sugar-bag slung over their backs, full of provisions to feed wives and children for another week in their lonely shacks. Such men became known as the Sugarbag Farmers. They were a familiar sight in the Dandenongs until the turn of the century, and a walking symbol of the rough existence these pioneer families were forced to lead.

Although the original State Forest was reduced to one fifth of its original size, the rest of the Dandenongs remained a fairly primitive rural area until the twentieth century. Then the lives of the people there were changed by the growth of modern transport. The nature of the Dandenongs was also changed. Having been transformed once from wild forest to rough bush selections, it was transformed again to a tourist and holiday area, within easy access of the great city of Melbourne.

The first step in this second transformation was the opening of the narrow gauge railway line from Upper Ferntree Gully to Gembrook. Back in 1900 when 'Puffing Billy', the little steam train that operated on this line, first came hissing and belching around the mountain curves, some early settlers were so terrified that they ran for their lives. Living wild in the hills like billygoats, there were many children who'd never seen a train. There were many who'd never been to Melbourne, and some who'd never been to school. 'Puffing Billy' changed all that. It brought Melbourne within easy reach of the Dandenongs. And, more importantly for the future of the mountains, it brought the Dandenongs within easy reach of Melbourne. The old days, when a trip from the city to the mountains involved a two-day ordeal in a horse and cart along bullock tracks, were gone forever.

The day of the mountain guesthouse had arrived at the Dandenongs. Tourists, eager for a breath of fresh air and anxious to escape from the growing noise and bustle and confinement of Melbourne, were drawn by the magnet of the Dandenongs, as they were also drawn in this period to the Mount Buffalo Chalet, and (for escapees from Sydney) to the grand hotels of the Blue Mountains.

Similar institutions sprang up in the Dandenongs to cater for this trade. One of the best-known and best-loved was Quamby at Olinda. Originally a tea-shop, it expanded to a guesthouse to accommodate the growing demand for accommodation. It boasted an original Dandenongs name — botanist Daniel Bunce had recorded in his notes of the 1840s that he established a camp 'on a rise of the mountain behind which flowed a small gurgling brook with banks lined with treefern Billarderia and which the blacks call Quambee Jack'.

It also boasted a particular kind of homely attraction and friendliness which kept its guests coming back for more, year after year. Mrs Iris Woolrich, whose family ran Quamby in those years, recalls that strawberries and cream, Devonshire teas and substantial roasts were all favoured items on the menu.

After tea in the dining room, they would roll back the lino for the guests to dance the hours away, or else to gather around the piano and sing the popular songs of the period, like 'Goodbye Dolly Gray', Mrs Woolrich remembers that Quamby even had its own special song:

'Quamby, dear old Quamby
With your scones so fresh and hot
And your coffee always boiling
And your lamingtons and your beautiful lemon
*   sponge*
Quamby, at Olinda
We will always think of you
Good old Quamby
Dear old Quamby
Can you blame anyone for falling in love with you?'

There were plenty of other institutions like it — Rostrevor, Hiawatha, Bella Vista, Kalorama, Shiloah — each with its devoted following. Until the 1920s, travel on the last stage of the journey, from the railway station to the guesthouse, was still by coach. Old coachmen like Tom Brown, who drove in the Dandenongs sixty years ago, recall that the trips were often quite hair-raising, especially when coming down the mountains on wet tracks, but the tourists loved every minute of it and would shout and sing their hearts out and make the loudest racket they could manage. They were not drunk; the guesthouses were abstemious places in those days. Tom says they were just suffering from mountain joy.

As the motor-car came into vogue and sealed roads began to appear in the mountains, the Dandenongs also came into vogue as a weekend retreat for the richer gentry of Melbourne. But such people didn't stay at guesthouses; they built their own. Some of the grand Dandenongs establishments which now operate as guesthouses or restaurants, such as Kenloch at Olinda, were originally erected as country houses for wealthy Melbourne manufacturers and merchants.

It was automatic for such people to ape the English style of doing things, and they attempted to create places where they and their select band of guests could enjoy the illusion that they were spending the weekend at a country house in Surrey. This was not such a bad thing for the Dandenongs. Quite a few of the original ten-acre selectors were happy enough to sell out at a profit and drift back to Melbourne where they found it easier to make a living. And rich people could afford more than one ten-acre block. Often they would buy four or five adjoining blocks and combine them into a single estate replete with ponds, fountains, and exotic gardens landscaped in the English style.

We might now wish that the people of those days had placed more value on the Australian trees like peppermint, messmate, yellow box and wattle, the undergrowth of dogwood, manuka, fern and Christmas bush, and the sixty varieties of wildflower native to the Dandenongs, including the heath, the bush violet, and the wax-lip orchid, sun orchid, spider orchid, helmet orchid and butterfly orchid. But, except in those areas like Sherbrooke Forest which were retained as part of the much larger original State Forest, the chance to preserve the Dandenongs as pure Australian scenery was gone long before 1920.

Instead, the Dandenongs had become a quite different scene, almost European both in appearance and scale. It was a patchwork of gardens and nurseries and small farms where every sort of exotic growth blossomed, and every variety of stone-fruit grew to ripeness and perfection. Carl Nobelius, a Finn, had established the first nursery at Emerald in the 1890s and launched the Dandenongs into a role it still plays as the nursery and flower-garden of Melbourne. By 1914, Nobelius had two million fruit-trees in 450 acres of nursery. Berry-growing was an established industry around Monbulk by the 1890s. The Monbulk Co-operative Fruit-growers Association was launched in 1897, and the first commerical production of jam began in 1914, an industry that made the name of Monbulk well known in many countries.

While the Dandenongs was now a quite different place to the 'Tanjenong' that the Wurundjeri tribe had known, it was not an unattractive place. On the contrary, the air was clean, the climate was healthy and the luxurious abundance of orchards and flower nurseries and vegetable gardens presented a pleasing picture to the eye. So did the gardens of the rich, with their elegant imported trees and their hedges, carefully trimmed by platoons of gardeners. But rich men don't usually get that way by being sentimentalists. And while there were a few who would rather have cut their throats than give up their country houses and vast gardens, there were plenty more who tired of playing the squire, or found it a life-style that didn't pay them enough profit. They agitated for permission to subdivide their properties and, unfortunately, they got it.

It was the most destructive thing to happen to the Dandenongs since the original decision to carve up the State Forest, and its effects are still being felt by local councils. There are, by now, plenty of councillors in the mountains who can see the danger of the Dandenongs being turned into just another suburb of Melbourne. Their battle, and one they have to fight with insufficient money and insufficient power, is to convince people that they should not build inappropriate suburban boxes on ludicrously small subdivisions. The problem is that the subdivisions were approved half a century ago and there are many of them still waiting to be built on.

A glance at a few of the real estate notices of the 1920s gives some indication of the speculative mania that overtook the Dandenongs. An advertisement for eighty mountain home sites at Selby in 1923 bellowed: 'Selby is developing fast, and values must rise. Buy First and Take Your Profit!' (This from a developer who had already subdivided the estate and taken *his* profit.) The advertisement promised 'The development of Selby must follow the same lines as the development of Belgrave.' One only has to look at Belgrave today, its street of suburban shops choked with traffic, and the beautiful old house of Dr Elef Jorgensen overshadowed and

below: **Dr Elef Jorgensen in his house at Belgrave**

menaced by supermarket blocks, to see what the Selby sale approach was leading to.

At Mount Upway Estate in 1927 '150 Weekend Home Blocks' were advertised for sale as 'the last holding of the Choicest Building Land in these Ranges'. Terms were easy — £2 deposit per lot and thereafter £1 a month. The sale was appropriately held on Boxing Day: many of these lots were destined to be occupied by little boxes built of ticky-tacky, and they all looked just the same.

I don't think it is elitist or inhumane to say that subdivisions into quarter-acre blocks should never have been allowed in the Dandenongs, and that the people who wanted to build suburban cottages on them should have been told to look elsewhere. There was tremendous pressure for land from the swollen city of Melbourne, but land was available to the north and the west and the south of the city — land that could have been subdivided without ruining a natural beauty spot.

Certainly it was pleasant for those people who gained their little weekend lots. Some found it so pleasant that they soon made the Dandenongs their permanent residence and took to commuting to the city. But the gain and the pleasure won by these individuals should have been measured against the loss suffered by the whole community every time another view of bush or farmland was blocked out by the shape of a suburban cottage. The scenic diversity that had been introduced by the cultivation of the land was one thing; the suburban uniformity created by streets of homes was quite another.

The Aboriginal name for these ranges meant 'a desirable and attractive place, replete with birds flying, kangaroos jumping, and lyrebirds singing'. Despite some of our worst efforts, it is still a desirable and attractive place, full of beauty and interest. There may not be so many kangaroos jumping around nowadays, but lyrebirds can still be seen in Sherbrooke Forest, the most beautiful native forest remaining in the Dandenongs. Noble stands of the mountain ash may also be seen there, as well as blackwood, grey gum, silver wattle, musk, sassafras and fern. The other remaining

top right: **Sculpture by William Ricketts**

right: **Puffing Billy**

natural areas of the ranges — Ferntree Gully National Park, Olinda Forest Reserve, Kalorama Park and Doongalla Reserve — are still reasonably replete with such birds as parrots, cockatoos, bellbirds, honey-eaters, whip birds and fairy wrens.

Amongst the introduced attractions of the mountains are the numerous nurseries and gardens ablaze in spring with tulips, rhododendrons, azaleas and camellias. Some of the great rambling 'informal' gardens of the Dandenongs also remain, at places like Folly Farm and the Cairnmillar Research Institute Garden. This style of garden, combining a blend of native and exotic trees — wattles and beeches clumped together, mountain ash and birch close alongside — was perfected by the landscape gardeners, Edna Walling and Ellis Stones, in the 1930s. It is a characteristic of these mountains as we now know them. It blends with the look of the place whereas the cramped geometric gardens, imported from the suburbs with their straight paths and square flower beds, stick out like sore thumbs. Variety is life to the Dandenongs; uniformity is death.

There is plenty of variety in the life styles of the Dandenongs people, and has been since the original village settlers and free selectors swarmed into the mountains. They were an exotic blend of Scots, Irish, French, Scandinavian, German and Dutch. Their backgrounds were as various as doctor, gold-digger, sea-captain and wharf-labourer. If anything, the area is even more cosmopolitan now and the cuisine offered by the forty Dandenongs guesthouses and restaurants includes Olde English, Dutch, Austrian, Jewish and Chinese. There are a dozen art galleries, a couple of theatres, and the hills are alive with potters, painters, woodcarvers, enamellers, goldsmiths, silversmiths, puppet-makers and authors.

As well as the parks, reserves, gardens, nurseries and flower markets that draw tourists from the city, there is Puffing Billy, a very popular attraction since it was restored in 1962 by local railway enthusiasts. Now it regularly chugs along the narrow track between Belgrave and Emerald Lake, its carriages packed with ecstatic kids of all ages.

There is also the William Ricketts sanctuary near Mount Dandenong where the sculptor Ricketts has carved a rockscape of Aboriginal figures that blend mystically into nature. Perhaps too many people gaze on these sculptures as curiosities, without understanding what Ricketts is trying to say. His work is really a cry of despair. He believes that we have lost the affinity and mystical reverence for the landscape that was the basis of Aboriginal life, and that the Dandenong Range itself is a glaring example of our neglect and ignorance.

We would do well to heed that warning. The Dandenong Range is not merely the lungs of Melbourne, it is the escape from Melbourne. It represents, or it should represent, everything that is *not* Melbourne. It is an invaluable asset, to Melbourne and to all Australia, but it is not an inexhaustible asset.

The tourists who come to enjoy themselves in the Dandenongs at the rate of 100 000 a year (and that number is doubling every six years) perhaps don't realise that the charm of the scenery is not as permanent as it looks. The population of the mountains has also doubled in fifteen years, from thirty thousand to sixty thousand. It's been estimated that even if not a single additional subdivision were allowed in the Dandenongs, those already approved could cause the population to rise to 135 000 and much of the development would be along the scenic roads that the tourists now travel.

It can't be allowed to happen. If it does, the whole of the Dandenongs will become just another suburban housing estate, paved over with tar and cement. The choice is between a housing estate for the thousands, or a vital breathing space for the millions. If it goes the way of the housing estate, Australia will lose another of its beautiful places. And in twenty years' time, even the people who were so keen to rush to a new life in the Dandenongs will find it hard to remember why they went in the first place.

opposite: **Fremantle Wharf, Swan River**

FREMANTLE

William Dampier saw the west coast of Australia in 1688. He comprehensively damned the land and its people and that was the last English word on the subject for well over a century. In the meantime, men of other nationalities visited the coast and found more alluring prospects than anything Dampier had been able to see at Buccaneer's Archipelago. Down towards the southern end of the coast, the Dutchman Willem de Vlamingh in 1697 found beautiful black swans on a river which became known in consequence as the Swan.

In 1801, a French expedition led by Hamelin and de Freycinet anchored at the mouth of the Swan and explored some of the country to the inland. The apparent interest of the French in this territory was much on the mind of Captain James Stirling when, in 1827, he came to the Swan River and explored it to the foothills of the Darling Ranges.

Stirling wrote a glowing report of the locality. He said:

'The richness of the soil, the bright foliage of the shrubs, the majesty of the surrounding trees, the abrupt and red-coloured banks of the river occasionally seen, and the view of the blue summits of the mountains from which we were not far distant, made the scenery round this spot as beautiful as anything of the kind I had ever witnessed.'

Charles Fraser, the Colonial Botanist for New South Wales, who accompanied Stirling on this trip, added his own eulogy of the area, concluding:

'I hesitate not in pronouncing it superior to any I have seen in New South Wales eastward of the Blue Mountains, not only in its local situation, but in the many advantages which it holds out to settlers.'

The settlers were soon to come, and when they found that Swan River was not an earthly paradise they had harsh things to say about those enthusiastic reports by Stirling and Fraser. But, at the time they were written, there were more urgent motives behind them than the alleged charms of the Swan River countryside. The British had already claimed possession of two-thirds of the Australian continent; all of this territory being known at that time as New South Wales.

But there remained one-third of the continent, a million square miles of land and over four thousand miles of coastline, in the west. It was feared that the French would lay claim to this territory and wreck the chance for the British to control the entire continent. Governor Darling had already tried to forestall this possibility by sending a detachment of troops and convicts under Major Edmund Lockyer to King George's Sound, on the south coast, in 1826. At a settlement which was supposed to be called Frederickstown, but instead became known as Albany, Lockyer's mission was to signify that the British had taken possession, by occupation, of the western part of the continent.

Apparently Governor Darling feared that the Albany settlement on its own was not a sufficient deterrent to French ambitions. On receipt of Stirling's report Darling sent off a despatch to London, stating:

'As Captain Stirling's visit to Swan River may attract attention and the report find its way into the French papers, it appears desirable, should His Majesty's Government entertain any intention of forming a settlement at that place, that no time should be lost in taking the necessary steps.'

His Majesty's Government, as it happened, was not entertaining any intention of forming a settlement at that place unless it could be done at no cost to itself. The feeling in Whitehall was that the Australian colonies had been a considerable drain on the British Exchequer for forty years and that to pour more money down the funnel would be madness. The first response from London dampened Darling's hopes of forestalling the French and Stirling's ambition to be the Governor of a new colony at Swan River.

But the situation changed in the middle of 1828. Sir George Murray, a friend of Stirling's, took over the Colonial Office Ministry and evinced some interest in the Swan River scheme if it could be managed at minimal expense to the British Government. Thomas Peel, a relative of the Home Secretary, Sir Robert Peel, then came forward with a proposal to settle 10 000 people at Swan River within four years in return for the grant of four million acres to his syndicate.

The Colonial Office was not so generous as that; but it offered Peel one million acres to be taken up over twenty-one years, conditional on the due arrival of settlers and the investment of agreed sums of money, and the completion of improvements on the land. Peel accepted these conditions and on December 30, 1828, Sir George Murray informed Stirling of His Majesty's Government's decision to form a settlement at the mouth of the Swan River. Stirling was to be the Lieutenant-Governor and would select the site for a capital, allocate land to the settlers and reserve a grant of 100 000 acres of land for himself.

While Stirling was preparing for his departure and Thomas Peel was rushing about frantically trying to enlist capitalists and labourers in his colonisation scheme, orders were given to the British naval commander at the Cape of Good Hope to despatch a ship to New Holland and annex the west coast, just in case the French should get any ideas before Stirling arrived.

Captain Charles Howe Fremantle was sent on this mission in the frigate *Challenger* and on May 2, 1829, Fremantle hoisted the Union Jack on the south head of the Swan River and took formal possession of the whole of the west coast of New Holland in the name of His Britannic Majesty. Fremantle did two important things that day: he completed the British annexation of Australia, leaving no legal foothold on the continent for the French, the Dutch, or, for that matter, the Aborigines; and he marked by his ceremony the site of a future city which was to be named for him.

Fremantle was still there with the *Challenger* at the end of May when Stirling and his party arrived in the *Parmelia*. Despite frantic signalling from Fremantle's men, Stirling tried to bring his ship in between Garden Island and the mainland and drove her on the rocks. The passengers had to be taken off and they spent the next few days in miserable weather on Garden Island. Some of the women and children were taken on board the *Challenger* and Fremantle noted that they transformed his cabin into a perfect pigsty until he grew impatient with their caterwauling and unceremoniously turned them all out.

Captain Fremantle waited about for two months, making surveys of Cockburn Sound and lending assistance to the administration.

But his primary role, as guard of the infant settlement, was superseded once HMS *Sulphur* arrived, and at the end of August the *Challenger* sailed away for India. Only once, three years later, did he ever return to take a look at the port which Stirling named in his honour.

However, the port of Fremantle bore an appropriate name. Captain Fremantle himself was a salty old seadog who had joined the navy in 1812, when he was twelve years old, and served as a midshipman at the blockade of New Orleans in 1814. A quarter of a century after the foundation of the Swan River settlement, Captain Fremantle was still in active service, organising the shipping and transport in Balaclava Harbour during the Crimean War. The son of a knight and an admiral, he eventually became a knight and an admiral himself, and commander-in-chief of the Channel Fleet at Portsmouth.

The West Australian town named for him was from the beginning a seadog's town. The tang of salt was always in the air and the sight of billowing sails was visible from every quarter. Later, when the rocky bar at the mouth of the river was blasted away to allow access to the big steamers, Fremantle became a bustling port city, one that the old Captain could have been proud of. And now, because it has managed to retain so much of its early architecture and its maritime atmosphere, Fremantle is a city that every Australian can be proud of.

Back at the beginning of the Swan River settlement, there was not too much pride about, either at Fremantle or at the spot further up the river which Stirling chose for his capital, and named Perth as a compliment to Sir George Murray, who was born at Perth in Scotland. Many of the early English settlers in Australia, especially those who took part in the idealistic colonisation schemes in South and West Australia, appear to have entertained the idea that they were going to a country where money would fall into their pockets without requiring any labour on their part. No doubt the arguments that were used to enrol them in these various schemes included unreal pictures of the ease and great prospects of life in colonial society. Then when these people arrived in Australia, after months of being tossed about in the huge swells of the Indian

Ocean and torn by the gales of the Roaring Forties, the very rigours of the trip had raised their expectations even higher. A country that required such effort to reach *must* be an Earthly Paradise.

Their first sight of the settlements, which were either totally unformed or else, in Macquarie's words, 'barely emerging from infantile imbecility', came as a dreadful shock to the immigrants. And the appearance of the countryside, so harsh, sunbaked and arid, so unlike any land that fell within their European experience, dashed their dreams to the ground so hard that some were shattered forever at the very first glimpse of Australia. Those who suffered this fate went about in a kind of stupor. Robbed of the impulse to action, they gloomed around the tents and the grog-shanties, cursing the heat, the flies, the mosquitoes and the Fates.

George Fletcher Moore, who arrived at Fremantle on the *Cleopatra* in 1830, recorded his first impression of the port as:

'A bare barren-looking district of sandy coast; the shrubs cut down for fire wood, the herbage trodden bare, a few wooden houses, many ragged-looking tents and contrivances for habitations, — our hotel a poor public-house into which everyone crowded, — our colony, a few cheerless dissatisfied people with gloomy looks, plodding their way through the sand from hut to hut to drink grog, and grumble out their discontents to each other.'

below: **The Gate, Fremantle Prison**

above right: **The Chapel, Fremantle Prison**

below right: **The Cell Block, Fremantle Prison**

Two years later, Moore again inspected Fremantle, and found a marked difference in the place:

'Now there is a town laid out in regular streets of stone houses with low walls, and in some places palisades in front; two or three large, well-kept inns or hotels, in which you can get clean beds and good private rooms. The soil there is loam resting upon a stratum of easily worked limestone and possessing a fertility almost beyond belief, with abundant water near the surface.'

Other observers agreed that Fremantle was making visible progress. Captain Fremantle himself, revisiting the town in 1832, considered that it was 'making really a very respectable show . . . I have no doubt, if the Colony continues, of its being in time a place of consequence'. He noted that it was making better progress than Perth, where very few houses had been built 'and many of those scarcely worthy of the name'.

No doubt the Captain felt some proprietorial interest in the town that bore his name, but there were many others who felt that the capital had been wrongly sited. Western Australia became the only Australian State where the capital city was not also the chief port, and it was strongly held for many years, particularly by the citizens of Fremantle, that this was a mistake that should be reversed. Time eventually made this controversy meaningless. Perth expanded to envelop Fremantle geographically, although it never subdued the independent rule or the local spirit of the port city.

By 1833, Fremantle was evincing symptoms of European civilisation. It had published its first two newspapers and had witnessed its first duel. This arose from bad feeling between William Clark, a solicitor, and George Johnson, a merchant, and it was instigated when Clark approached Johnson in the street and issued the peculiar challenge: 'Sir, you are a scoundrel and a blackguard, and if it was not from motives of prudence, I would give you a sound drubbing.' Johnson sent a second to respond to the challenge and a pistol duel was fought at sunrise next morning in a Fremantle paddock. Clark was the better shot and Johnson fell with a bullet in his side and bled to death. Clark was tried for murder, but acquitted. Fortified by this early experience in combat, he went on to become proprietor and editor of the *Swan River Guardian*.

Fremantle also had by 1833 the beginnings of an ambitious town plan and its first notable public building. Both were the work of the mysterious H. W. Revely, whom Stirling had picked up in Table Bay during the voyage out and enrolled as his Civil Engineer. On Arthur Head, where Captain Fremantle had first raised the British flag in 1829, Revely supervised the construction in 1831 of an impressive twelve-sided edifice, built from local limestone and designated (inexactly) the Round House.

The Round House was an extraordinarily ambitious building for such a young settlement, and one of the mysteries concerning Revely is how he was able to get permission to proceed with this plan. Built to dominate the western end of the High Street, and built before the High Street even existed, the Round House is one of Australia's most significant buildings. No other Australian capital can point to so noble a building to mark the place, and virtually the time, of the colony's formation.

Beautifully restored now to its original condition, the Round House is Western Australia's oldest public building, and the only building in Fremantle to remain complete and intact from the pre-convict era. It was itself a gaol — in fact, it was the local lock-up — but it was not the kind of gaol with which Fremantle later became associated. Western Australia was originally promoted as a free colony. One of its chief attractions to settlers was supposed to be its distance, and its difference, from the squalid convict societies of Eastern Australia. And so the Round House was built with only eight cells. The Colony was not anticipating trouble from any criminal elements.

But the Colony struck trouble of a different kind, economic trouble, and was eventually forced to change its mind on the convict question. Captain Fremantle had wisely added, to his prediction that Fremantle would become 'a place of Consequence', the qualification 'if the Colony continues.' For twenty years after its foundation there was a real doubt whether the Colony *would* continue. Some never doubted it. G. F. Moore had composed as early as 1831, one year after his arrival, an unofficial anthem which he rendered at a Government House ball given by Captain Stirling and his wife in Perth. His song enthused:

'With care and experience, I'm sure 'twill be found
Two crops in the year we may get from the ground,
There's good wood and good water, good flesh and
good fish
Good soil and good clime, and what more could you
wish.
Then let everyone earnestly strive, Sirs
Do his best, be alert and alive, Sirs,
We'll soon see our colony thrive, Sirs,
So Western Australia *for me.'*

But Moore had been lucky enough to obtain good land on the Swan at Guildford, where his vegetables prospered; and he was by nature an optimist. Others were not so sure. Too many things seemed to be going wrong. Thomas Peel struck disaster right from the outset when the ship *Rockingham,* with his settlers on board, was wrecked on the coast. His planned estate broke up for want of capital and labour and he was left, like many others, squatting on large but unproductive tracts of land.

Western Australia's worst problem was the lack of people, that is white people. The settlers, typical of their time, regarded the Aborigines as belonging to the animal rather than the human kingdom. After the first couple of years, British settlers could not be enticed to the Swan. By 1837 the white population was only 2 000, including 600 at Perth and 400 at Fremantle. By 1850, when the colony was glumly celebrating its twenty-first birthday, there were only 7 000 whites in the whole of Western Australia. Some of the keener-eyed gentry, like the Henty family, had arrived, concluded that the high social standing offered to them in this free colony would not compensate for the lack of labour and economic opportunity, and had moved on to the convict East. Eventually Western Australia drew the moral from this and similar moves and swallowed its pride. In 1850 the old system of transportation was on its last legs. New South Wales and Van Diemen's Land had already signified to the British

Government that they would take in no more convicts. At this moment, Western Australia applied to take them in, and so commenced its career as the last of the Australian penal colonies.

It was a step that dented the settlers' self-esteem but worked wonders for the economy. The arrival of a cheap labour force (a slave labour force, in fact) ensured that Western Australia would continue and all talk of abandoning the colony ceased. The results of the convicts' labours can still be seen in some of the West's most prominent landmarks, and most notably in Fremantle itself, where it was decided to house the prisoners.

The first job given to the convicts was to build their own gaol, on a hill in Fremantle, from limestone quarried locally at North Fremantle. Captain Henderson, the Comptroller-General of the Convict Establishment, selected the site and designed a huge complex of cellblocks, stores, offices, guardrooms and warder's cottage. There was a massive Main Block, with a Chapel, a feature regarded as very important in the penal thinking of the time. A penitentiary was a place where men were to be taught to repent, and the Chapel was the place for them to do their repenting in. Attendance was compulsory. There was a hospital block, a kitchen block, and an imposing entrance building which formed a part of the huge wall. The whole project covered fourteen acres and was designed to hold 1 000 convicts. It took seven years to build, from 1851, and it cost so much money that the British Government, which had to bear the cost, was forever imploring Henderson to economise and to stop thinking so big.

But the gaol was meant to last, and it did. Unlike the other visible remains of the British Colonial Convict Establishments at Port Arthur and Norfolk Island, Fremantle Prison never fell into ruins, and never fell out of use as a gaol. Ten thousand convicts, all of them male, were sent across the sea to Fremantle between 1851 and 1868 when the transportation system was abandoned. Not until 1886, however, was the control passed from the Imperial to the Colonial authorities. The prison remains as Western Australia's biggest, currently housing some 500 prisoners. It is thought to be the only British Colonial

Convict Establishment in the world which stands intact and still operates as a prison.

The convicts at Fremantle contributed greatly to the architecture of the town, and they also contributed greatly to its legends. Amongst the relics of the convict days that can still be inspected there — straitjackets, leg-irons, the whip and the flogging pole, and the cell of a transported convict named Walsh, decorated with the most remarkable Biblical illustrations which he contrived with a pencil and coloured with cocoa powder — is the cell of Western Australia's only noted bushranger, Moondyne Joe. As a bushranger, Moondyne Joe hardly ranks with Ned Kelly, Dan Morgan or Ben Hall — he never killed a policeman or robbed a bank or coach, and he didn't even carry a gun. But as an escapologist, he was in the Houdini class. His real name was Joseph Bolitho Johns and he was a Welshman, transported to Western Australia in the *Pyrenees* in 1852 when he was twenty-two years old. He was conditionally pardoned a couple of years later and made his way to Moondyne Springs in the Darling Ranges where he commenced a career as a horse trader.

Joe's method of trading was unconventional. He trapped the local settlers' horses at their watering-holes and then returned them to their grateful owners, claiming a reward for his trouble. It was noticed that the high incidence of horses straying coincided with Joe's arrival in the district. In 1861 he was caught at the game, arrested and put in gaol. He immediately escaped, in the first of a long series of apparently effortless escapes that earned him increasingly severe sentences. There came a time when nobody could remember what Moondyne Joe's original crime was. They only knew that he faced a lifetime in prison for the crime of escaping from prison — and Joe could always be counted on to compound the sentence by escaping again.

Discipline at Fremantle Prison under its first two Comptroller-Generals, Captain Henderson and Captain Newlands, was mild, but in 1866, when Governor Hampton took over the colony, he resolved to make a change. Hampton had previously been Comptroller-General of

below: **The Courtyard, Fremantle Museum, formerly The Lunatic Asylum**

above: House of Sir Frederick Samson, Fremantle

right: History preserved in the Samson House

below: Mrs Laurie, sister of Sir Frederick Samson

Prisons in Tasmania where the chain gang and the lash were the standard methods of dealing with convicts.

Hampton appointed his own son as Acting Comptroller-General of Prisons, and instructed him to introduce the Tasmanian methods. The pair of them were especially resolved to make an example of Moondyne Joe, whose constant escapes were drawing ridicule on the prison system. Joe was put in irons and confined to a cell in Fremantle Prison. A few months later he was found to be in possession of a file and a pocket-knife, with which he had almost carved the lock out of his cell door. Despite Joe's indignant protestations, his gaol-breaking kit was taken away and he was transferred to a special high-security cell where he was chained to the wall. Joe then complained that there was no ventilation in his cell and the prison authorities agreed to remove one small pane of glass from the window. On the night of August 6, 1866, Joe escaped through that hole in the window. It was never discovered how he had freed himself of his chains.

He returned to his old stamping grounds, in the bush around Moondyne Springs, and he was recaptured there a couple of months later. This time, Joe was wrapped in chains like a mummy, while carpenters at Fremantle Prison laboured for several days, under the express instruction of Governor Hampton, to create a cell from which escape would be impossible.

That cell has been preserved at Fremantle Prison as a relic of the convict days, and it can still be inspected. The carpenters lined the walls with thick timber boards and secured them to the stone with steel railway dogspikes to prevent Joe prising away the timber and tunnelling through the stone. The window was given additional layers of steel bars and metal-plated all around so that the bars could never be loosened. Originally it was proposed to attach Joe by chains to a ringbolt secured in the iron-studded walls, but Governor Hampton was convinced that Joe could never escape from this cell, which was very much like a tomb both in atmosphere and scale. He went so far as to promise Joe his liberty if he managed to escape again.

It was a rash promise. Moondyne Joe languished in his dark and airless cell, on a diet of bread and water, until medical authorities at the prison said he would die without fresh air and exercise. Joe was then permitted into the prison yard to break a heap of enormous rocks under the supervision of a special sentry. The sentry ended up on good terms with Joe, and one afternoon, noticing that the convict had collapsed on the other side of the rockheap with his hat still on and his pick in his hand, he decided to let the poor devil sleep on. When the time came to escort Joe back to his cell, the sentry discovered that he had been guarding a dummy, shaped out of a prisoner's shirt, trousers and boots, filled with rubble, and crowned with a hat and a pick. In the prison wall behind the rockheap, a freshly dug hole gaped. Moondyne Joe, in his drawers and prison socks, had bolted through the hole, and through the prison superintendent's garden, and was at large again.

This time, Joe kept his freedom for nearly two years, after which he was recaptured in Mr Ferguson's wine cellar at Middle Swan just as he was about to sample the vintage that he intended to take off the vigneron's hands. Governor Hampton had left the colony a year before and Joe's protest, that he had won his liberty fair and square, by beating the Governor's challenge, was ignored. He was kept in prison, but under more humane conditions, until the 1870s. His later life is unknown although it is rumoured that he lived till he was ninety, and died in an Old Men's Home. But he had become immortal in Western Australian legend because of his famous underwear escape, and the Hamptons, father and son, must have gnashed their teeth whenever they heard the scornful little ditty that was sung in Fremantle:

'The Governor's son has got the pip,
The Governor's got the measles
'Cause Moondyne Joe has give 'em the slip
Pop goes the weasel!'

Ten years later, another song became popular in Fremantle — too popular, in the opinion of the colonial Government which attempted to suppress the singing of this song in taverns. The authorities claimed that it was seditious and corrosive to good government — they might have added that it made them out to be such perfect fools. Again it was a song about an escape from Fremantle Prison, and one that put even Moondyne Joe's escapades in the shade. It was the biggest mass gaolbreak in West Australian history, and probably the neatest trick that was ever pulled on the Australian convict system.

The last ship to carry convicts to Australia, the *Hougemont,* arrived at Fremantle on January 10, 1868. Included in its cargo of convicts were thirty-eight Fenians, Irish political prisoners who had been transported for the crime of opposing British rule in their country. Some of them were still languishing in Fremantle Prison seven years later, but by then their plight had reached the ears of Fenian sympathisers in America and a plan had been launched to rescue them. A number of people were responsible for setting up the plan, which took two years and a small fortune to bring off and which almost created an international crisis in the process. But two men were chiefly responsible for its execution — John J. Breslin, an Irishman, and Captain Anthony, the American Commander of the whaleship *Catalpa.*

Breslin arrived in Fremantle in November 1875, under the assumed name of Captain Collins, and spent the next five months setting up the escape through a Fenian ex-prisoner who had contact with the six Fenians who were still captives. By this time all of them had become trusties through their good conduct and were regularly sent on day labour outside the gaol. Early on the morning of Perth Regatta Day, Easter Monday, 1876, as the Fenians left the Fremantle Prison to march to their work, they were snatched up by two horse traps, driven by Breslin and an accomplice, and hustled down to Rockingham. There, a whaleboat was waiting to take them out to the *Catalpa,* which had been purchased by the American Fenians and sent to rescue them.

The escape was discovered and the whaleboat was almost intercepted by the coastal steamer *Georgette* before the Fenians managed at last to board the *Catalpa.* Once on board they breathed easy, but they were not clear yet. Feverish overnight work at Fremantle, under the instructions of the Governor, transformed the *Georgette* into a man-of-war, with a twelve-pound howitzer on board.

The next day, with the power of her steam engines, the *Georgette* ran down the sailing-ship *Catalpa* while she was still in Western Australian waters and demanded that the convicts be given up. But Captain Anthony denied any knowledge of convicts on board. (As far as he was concerned, they were now free men.) When the *Georgette* threatened to blow the *Catalpa's* masts away, Captain Anthony hoisted the Star-Spangled Banner and defied them to fire on the American flag. To do that would have been to risk a war with the United States. It was probably a remote risk, but the *Georgette* had been instructed not to take undue risks. She backed away and the *Catalpa* sailed away with her Fenian cargo to New Bedford, and freedom.

The incident became almost immediately the subject of a ballad called *The Catalpa.* It is the most mettlesome of all Australian convict ballads, perhaps not surprising since there was for once a genuine convict victory to celebrate:

'*A noble whaleship and commander, called the Catalpa, they say,*
Sailed out to Western Australia, and stole six bold Fenians away.

CHORUS:
Come all you screw warders and gaolers, remember Perth Regatta Day,
Take care of the rest of your Fenians, or the Yankees will steal them away.

For seven long years they had served here, and seven long more had to stay
For defending their country, old Ireland, for that they were banished away.

You kept them in Western Australia, till their hair had begun to turn grey
When a Yank from the States of America came out here and stole them away.

Now all the Perth boats were a-racing, and making hard tacks for the spot
But the Yankee tacked into Fremantle, and stole the best prize of the lot.

The Georgette, well-armed with bold warriors, went out the poor Yanks to arrest
But she hoisted her star-spangled banner, saying "You will not board me, I guess."

*Now they've landed safe in America, and there will
    be able to cry
"Hoist up the green flag and the shamrock, hurrah
    for old Ireland we'll die."
So remember those Fenians colonial, and sing all
    these verses with skill
And remember the Yankee that stole them, and the
    home that they left on the hill.'*

CHORUS

The home that the Fenians left on the hill was
gradually emptied of the rest of its transported
convicts, but it remains in Fremantle as one of
their two most striking memorials. The other
was the Lunatic Asylum, which the convicts
built after they'd finished the prison. It was just
as grim a place for human beings. Many of its
inmates were in fact convicts who had become
insane on the long voyage out from England,
and who, in the Asylum, were treated with the
utmost brutality. Any who weren't lunatics
when they were committed to the Asylum
must have become so shortly afterwards.

The Asylum was declared totally unfit for its
original purpose in 1909. Fremantle, by then,
had become a different place. The West
Australian goldrushes of the 1880s and 1890s
brought gold-seekers in their thousands. Many
of them arrived by ship at Fremantle and
many complained of the dangers of the
harbour where large ships were still forced to
anchor on the outside coast.

The engineering genius of the West, C. Y.
O'Connor, solved the problem by blasting
away the rock bar at the mouth of the Swan.
As soon as large steamships were able to enter
the river, Fremantle replaced Albany as the
first Australian port of call for the liners from
Europe. It became one of Australia's leading
ports, and it remains today as a bustling and
prosperous maritime city.

below: **The architecture of Fremantle**

right: **The Roundhouse and old Fremantle buildings**

below right: **Classic Fremantle style**

But unlike other Australian cities, where the usual equation was that 'progress' entailed the destruction of old buildings and the creation of new ones, Fremantle managed to retain a great deal of its past. There were some losses, but Fremantle can still boast the Round House and a few other buildings from its Free Settlement era, and a host of impressive and beautiful buildings from the convict and the goldrush eras. They combine to give Fremantle a spirit of harmony and historic integrity unique in Australian cities today.

This did not happen by accident. The same forces of development that destroyed the historic heart of older Australian cities were at work in Fremantle in the 1950s and 1960s. But Fremantle was lucky enough to have a Mayor, Sir Frederick Samson, who was descended from a pioneer family in the city, and who believed that the past was worth hanging on to. The turning point was the battle for the Fremantle Asylum. It had fallen into a state of dreadful disrepair and there were loud voices urging that it be demolished. The site was a very valuable one and money was, as usual, leading the loud chorus. But Sir Frederick Samson wasn't impressed. He liked to quote the motto of the city, which it borrowed from the Fremantle family, Nec prece nec pretio. It means 'neither by entreaty nor by bribery' and Sir Frederick publicly interpreted it as meaning 'the Council can't be bought'.

With his leadership, and with the support of many enthusiasts whose vision of Fremantle's unique value was not blinded by dollar signs, the Asylum was saved. Now, beautifully restored, it fulfils a useful purpose as a History Museum and Arts Centre and is boasted as Australia's finest example of Colonial Gothic.

So many fine buildings remain in Fremantle that there is no point in listing them individually. The point is that they remain not as individual curiosities, but as integral parts of an historic city, with its own special character and identity. It is not Australia's oldest city — it was founded forty-one years after Phillip arrived at Botany Bay — but in its treatment of the past, it represents everything that Botany Bay is not.

Two lessons can be derived from the story of Fremantle. One is that it is quite possible to preserve a city, with its colour and its legends, without turning it entirely into a museum or a stuffed exhibit in a glass case for the inspection of the curious. Fremantle is no recreated 'folk village'; it is a genuine, living, breathing city, which still manages to serve all the practical mercantile purposes for which it was founded, while yet remaining a city on a human scale, a place that people can identify with, enjoy living in, and feel proud of. And the way this was achieved was not by destroying the best of the old buildings, but by creative imagination, in adapting those old buildings to new uses.

The second lesson that Fremantle offers is that historic cities can't be saved by sentiment alone. It takes money as well, and the preservation of Fremantle has cost more money than could ever have been raised from the ratepayers of that city. It has been paid for by the Australian taxpayer. The National Estate program, in the years 1973 to 1976, granted half a million dollars towards the restoration of Fremantle. That amounts to a total contribution of four cents from every Australian, and for that we have saved a treasure-house of history. Instead we could have let Fremantle collapse into another great Australian eyesore, another visual outrage, another Botany Bay. And we could have saved our four cents.

There are some who would regard that as a useful economy and a good prescription for the future. I believe that we don't deserve a future, and are not likely to have one, if we cannot grasp the value of a proper respect for our own past. A lot of lives — great and small, black and white, right and wrong — have been expended in the making of Australia. We owe those people a greater debt than four cents.

CHECK LIST

General
A history of Australia: *C M H Clark*
A Continent Takes Shape: *Egon and Elsie Kunz*
Australian Encyclopaedia: *ed. A H Chisholm*
The Discovery and Exploration of Australia:
  E & G Feeken & O Spate
Australia — The First Hundred Years: *A Garran*
The Australian Colonists: *K S Inglis*
The Story of Australia: *A G L Shaw*

Botany Bay
A New Voyage Round the World:
  William Dampier
The Journals of Captain James Cook: *ed.*
  J. C. Beaglehole
A Narrative of the Expedition to Botany Bay:
  Watkin Tench
The Fatal Impact: *Alan Moorehead*
Sir Joseph Banks, The Father of Australia:
  J H Maiden
The History of Botany: *Frederick A Larcombe*

The Hawkesbury River
Extracts of Letters from Arthur Phillip to Lord
  Sydney: *A Phillip*
Macquarie's World: *Marjorie Barnard*
Macquarie Country: *D G Bowd*
Maquarie's Five Towns: *Olaf Ruhen*
A Companion Guide to Sydney: *Ruth Park*
The Sydney Guide Book: *Patricia Rolfe*

Follies
Architecture in Australia: *J M Freeland*
The Early Australian Architects: *Morton Herman*
They Came to a Valley: *D I McDonald*
History of Australian Land Settlement:
  S H Roberts
Ghost Towns of Australia: *George Farwell*
Australia's Western Third: *F H Crowley*

Ben Boyd
The Three Colonies of Australia: *S Sidney*
The Last Cruise of the Wanderer: *J Webster*
Discovering Monaro: *W K Hancock*
Benjamin Boyd in Australia: *H. P Wellings*
The Solomon Islands: *Janet Kent*
Australian Dictionary of Biography: *ed. Douglas Pike*

The Darling River
Two Expeditions into the Interior of Southern
  Australia: *Charles Sturt*
Three Expeditions into the Interior of Eastern
  Australia: *Thomas Mitchell*
Sturt of the Murray: *Michael Langley*
The History of Bourke: *Bourke Historical Society*
Riverboats: *Ian Mudie*
Riverboat Days: *Peter Phillips*

The Birdsville Track
Land of Mirage: *George Farwell*
Two Expeditions into Central Australia:
  Charles Sturt
Flying Fox and Drifting Sand: *Frances Ratcliff*
Australian Folklore: *W Fearn-Wannan*
Australia: *Griffith Taylor*
The Territory: *Ernestine Hill*

The Centre
Central Australia: *C T Madigan*
Brown Men and Red Sand: *C P Mountford*
Australia's Open North: *J MacDonald Holmes*
A Guide to Central Australia: *Jeff Carter*
Their Shining Eldorado: *Elspeth Huxley*
The Geology of Central Australia: *D R Woolley*

Arnhem Land
Journal of an Overland Expedition in Australia
  from Moreton Bay to Port Essington: *L Leichhardt*
Journals of the Australian Explorations:
  A C & F F Gregory
Arnhem Land: *R M & C H Berndt*
The World of the First Australians:
  R M & C H Berndt
Strange New World: *A H Chisholm*
Australia's North: *Stanley & Kay Breedon*

The Flinders Ranges
A Voyage to Terra Australis: *Matthew Flinders*
Robbery Under Arms: *Rolf Boldrewood*
The Story of the Flinders Ranges: *Hans Mincham*
The Rise and Fall of Beltana: *Ivan Hull*
Through the Northern Flinders Ranges: *Jocelyn Burt*
Range Without Men: *Colin Thiele*

Little Cornwall
South Australia and Its Mines: *Francis Dutton*
Early Experiences of Life in South Australia:
    J W Bull
The Mines of South Australia: *J B Austin*
Australia's Little Cornwall: *Oswald Pryor*
Men and Mines: *John Reynolds*
Australia's Earliest Mining Era: *Ian Auhl & Dennis Marfleet*

The Wild West Coast of Tasmania
For the Term of his Natural Life: *Marcus Clarke*
Old Tales of a Young Country: *Marcus Clarke*
Tales of the Convict System: *Price Warung*
The History of Tasmania: *John West*
The Story of the Australian Bushrangers: *G Boxall*
Convicts and the Colonies: *A G L Shaw*
The Convict Years: *Margaret Wiedenhofer*
The Peaks of Lyell: *Geoffrey Blainey*

The Dandenongs
Australasiatic Reminiscences: *Daniel Bunce*
The Overlander: *E J Brady*
Aboriginals of the Dandenong Mountains:
    Muriel McGivern
The Story of the Dandenongs: *Helen Coulson*
The Dandenongs: *Nettie Palmer*
The Day of My Soul: *William Ricketts*

Fremantle
A History of West Australia: *W B Kimberly*
The Mutiny of the Chains: *John Boyle O'Reilly*
Fremantle Mission: *Sean O'Laing*
The History of Fremantle: *J K Hitchcock*
The Western Gateway: *John K Ewers*
Unwilling Emigrants: *Alexandra Hasluck*